APOCALYPSE ANYTIME

An Interspiritual Devotional for a World on Fire

CAROLYN BAKER

APOCRYPHILE
PRESS

Apocryphile Press
PO Box 255
Hannacroix, NY 12087 www.apocryphilepress.com

Copyright © 2023 by Carolyn Baker
Printed in the United States of America
ISBN 978-1-958061-32-9 | paper
ISBN 978-1-958061-33-6 | ePub

Please join our mailing list at www.apocryphilepress.com/free. We'll keep you up-to-date on all our new releases, and we'll also send you a FREE BOOK. Visit us today!

CONTENTS

ALSO BY THE AUTHOR

- The Journey of Forgiveness
- Coming Out of Fundamentalist Christianity
- Sacred Demise
- Navigating The Coming Chaos
- Collapsing Consciously
- Collapsing Consciously Ebook Meditations
- Love in the Age of Ecological Apocalypse
- Return to Joy, with Andrew Harvey
- Dark Gold: The Human Shadow and the Global Crisis
- Savage Grace with Andrew Harvey
- Journey to the Promised Land: How a Homeless Stranger Took Me Home
- Saving Animals from Ourselves with Andrew Harvey
- Radical Regeneration with Andrew Harvey
- Confronting Christofascism: Healing the Evangelical Wound
- Undaunted: Living Fiercely into Climate Meltdown in an Authoritarian World

FOREWORD: A JOURNEY

BY ALISON HINE

We shall not cease from exploration
And the end of all our exploring
Will be to arrive where we started
And know the place for the first time.
—Little Gidding, TS. Eliot

The front cover of this book is visually arresting. Carolyn Baker weaves the flames of the Apocalypse emerging in our times into an ancient form of Christian literature, known as a Devotional. This is not a Christian Devotional, rather Carolyn Baker uses contemporary wisdom drawn from a wide landscape. This book is an alchemical encounter between the fires of chaos and breakdown married with the wisdom of our elders. The result is this interspiritual Devotional.

The earliest devotional, the *Felire*, was written in the ninth century in Ireland as a daily monastic practice. Interestingly, the word *Felire* has one of its roots in the Latin *vigil*, meaning watchfulness. Deep in the origins of this spiritual literature was a daily practice of spiritual reading. Running through this Devotional is the call into direct soul experiencing, an immersive embodied watchfulness. This is neither an intellectual study guide nor a self-help book.

Carolyn Baker begins her Devotional with the HBO series *The Last of Us*. I always steered clear of the horror of this dystopian and zombie genre. In her last book, *Undaunted: Living Fiercely into Climate Meltdown in an Authoritarian World,* Carolyn Baker introduces the reader to what she calls *fierce practices*, practices designed to challenge our complacency and denial, and to face our deepest fears and bottomless grief.

To test my courage, I decided to watch this series as such a fierce practice. Oh sure I flinched, covered my eyes, but gradually I was drawn into this powerful narrative. I began to wonder if in a world overrun by sheer survival, with all its savagery and ugliness, there was room for goodness and tenderness. And thankfully, we see human kindness and love, even if there are fearsome boundaries of protection made of landmines, barbed wire, heavily armed guards and fierce dogs. Maslow's hierarchy of needs reminds us that without basic protection, the possibility of kindness and generosity is difficult. And yet right at the center of this television series are the two main characters —a shell of a broken man and a raging teenage girl, both deeply traumatized, neither of them able to trust or respect each other. They are thrown unwillingly into the task of making their way across thousands of miles with no protection other than their intense need to get to their destination. Initially, all they possess are their sharply-honed instincts with a willingness and ability to kill to save each other. Gradually, exposed as they are to ever present danger, something deeply human grows between them, nothing sentimental, but a deep redemptive and healing love.

It is easy to think that only heroic figures like Nelson Mandela and Martin Luther King or Joan of Arc, are capable of the fierce practices of courage, resilience and loving service. The fact that you the reader have made it this far into this Devotional suggests that you are already involved in a deeper process, a psycho-spiritual journey of awakening in these apocalyptic times.

Through Carolyn Baker's Devotional there is an arc of inner soul development that follows the wisdom laid out at the beginning of the recently discovered Gospel of Thomas, found in a cliff near Nag Hammadi in the Egyptian desert in 1945. It contains a hundred and fourteen aphorisms or wisdom sayings of Yeshua (Jesus). Early in this text:

Yeshua (Jesus) says...
If you are searching, you must not stop until you find.
When you find, however, you will become troubled.
Your confusion will give way to wonder.
In wonder you will reign over all things.
Your sovereignty will be your rest.

ॐ

If you are searching, you must not stop until you find....

In these few lines Yeshua sets out the path of soul maturation and spiritual awakening. We begin our *search* out of some deep sense that something is missing. Maybe we are looking to heal some heartbreak within our hearts. Or maybe we are looking for a kind hope in order to face what seems like a hopeless future. Or maybe we need to find within ourselves some sustaining resilience? Or maybe we need to find somewhere below our fears the courage to face this civilizational crisis. Perhaps we need some means to find a meaningful way to act within a world where there seem to be no solutions to the spiraling crises. This Devotional offers a place to land, a place to *find* yourself, a place to begin a pilgrimage of sorts, a map of a landscape to find your footing. Page by page, Carolyn Baker takes us into this spiraling process of descent, discovery, wisdom, joy, compassion and maturity.

When you find, however, you will become troubled...

Carolynn Baker situates us rightly into *trouble*, in the seductive and slippery slope of hope. We have to face that our hope is really a naive optimism or a kind of magical, wishful thinking to escape fear. We cling to hope only to have it dashed. And so fear returns and we scramble to find a new source of hope. So it goes, back and forth between hope and fear until we realize that this hope creates a protective and numbing wall around our heart and grief that seems to have no bottom.

We are now drawn into the deepest *trouble*. This is a descent into the darkness of the unconscious and all that we have repressed—the trauma and all the losses. Here we may be tempted to skip over this, bypassing this pain in order to find an escape. Maybe AI, friendly aliens, or the Rapture will save us from disaster. But it is only in the Shadow where we will find the true ground of our humanity and the spiritual gold of our being. This journey into the underworld is not simply psychological; it is an earthy encounter with our most treasured gift—our precious heart. Stripped of her hardened walls, the heart begins to grieve for all that is being lost at the hands of the extractive greed of human activity. As this grief extends itself we encounter an unrelenting emptiness, an emptiness that cannot be filled by any of the consolations of our comfortable, material existence.

Your confusion will give way to wonder...

There is no hope and no fear, nothing to do but breathe and wait without expectation. And it is here that we may notice that this emptiness is not a gnawing sense of hollowness, but a subtle spaciousness. This is the portal to the *wonder* of our spiritual nature coming forward to touch us. The grief now turns into tears of gratitude as we awaken into a new experience of the world. The world now appears alive and precious. We see through our desecrated landscape into a living world, a conscious world. And now we know joy, not happiness in the midst of a world in trouble.

The US Constitution enshrines the pursuit of happiness as a foundational principle guiding this democracy. But happiness is ephemeral, entirely dependent on fulfilling the desires of our instinctual nature. We never cease from wanting, especially if it is glittery, yummy, and cool. And for a while we are happy, but then its allure fades and we start looking for the next something to fill our hollowness, boredom, and anxiety. This appetite will never be satisfied. Soon happiness becomes a deadening and unquenchable addiction.

In 2010 following an explosion on the oil rig the Deepwater Horizon, an oil spill spread out over the Gulf waters. This was the largest marine oil spill in history. I remember watching the images of oil rolling over the delicate marshes along the Gulf coast. My heart hurt. One morning during meditation I saw the oil seeping in among the marsh grasses and to my surprise, instead of horror I felt sweet love, followed by joy. This made no sense to me and I felt guilty about my insensitivity to the obvious suffering of the Gulf ecosystem and the local population.

It wasn't until much later that I realized directly that divine consciousness "lies below" or "beyond", or "through" the surface stream of my experiencing. No matter the content, if we have traversed to some degree, the descent—the realm of trouble, we will know this wonder, this joy of being. Joy brings a depth of meaning to the soul and a sense that we are here for a reason. We taste that it is possible to live in the midst of the crises without drowning in despair. Joy is not simply smiley and syrupy, it is radiant, it is zestful and it is grounded.

In wonder you will reign over all things.
Your sovereignty will be your rest.

It is this grounded lightness that draws our souls towards our particular expression in the world. We know what we are here to do. Right now in this moment just in front us, the next step appears, sometimes easy, sometimes trying, and sometimes we stumble. Something precious develops within us in this moment by moment encounter with what lies in front of us. Some call this preciousness a pearl of great price. It is the irritation of the grit of sand trapped in the oyster shell that produces the luminosity of the pearl. We also grow as we encounter the grit of life. If once again we try to avoid this maturation of the soul and seek to find more exciting spiritual highs, the glow of embodied wisdom cannot take root in our hearts. And we will cease to shine with joy and welcome.

Finally we are no longer desperate for the consolations of spirit. Instead we are offered up in service of care, healing and comfort for those we find around us. Oh sure we will fall down, make mistakes, bad things will happen and the world will continues to burn, but the life-giving flames are never far away. When we fall, we can now stand back up into our spiritual maturity. Wendell Berry calls this the practice of resurrection. Yeshua calls this sovereignty. Carolyn Baker calls this fierce practice.

It was only when I looked closely at the front cover of this book that I noticed that the flames enclosed a beautiful tulip. The tulip is at ease and at rest. These flames don't destroy. The flames have transformed her beauty into radiance. The tulip has become a blessing. And so it is for us.

This transformation reminds me of the last lines in *Little Gidding* by T.S.Eliot:

> *And all shall be well and*
> *All manner of thing shall be well*
> *When the tongues of flames are in-folded*
> *Into the crowned knot of fire*
> *And the fire and the rose are one.*

Alison Hine was raised in an intellectual, scientific, atheist family in Geneva, Switzerland. Her father was one of the founding scientists at CERN. She obtained a degree in zoology from Cambridge University. After some field work in Kenya and further academic studies in Canada, she settled in Ann Arbor, Michigan where she obtained a Master's degree in Social Work from the University of Michigan. She practiced as a psychotherapist for 35 years and began offering spiritual direction in 2005. Currently she is a priest and an abbot in the Oriental Orthodox Order in the West.

INTRODUCTION

In the first month of January, 2023, HBO Television premiered a new apocalyptic series called *The Last of Us.* Based on a 2013 video game, the series is set in 2023, twenty years into a global pandemic caused by a mass fungal infection, which forces its hosts to transform into zombie-like creatures. The series follows Joel (Pedro Pascal), a hardened middle-aged survivor tormented by the trauma of his past, who is tasked with smuggling a young girl, Ellie (Bella Ramsey), out of a quarantine zone and across the United States. The series is essentially about their odyssey.

I do not wish to offer any series spoilers, but while most television writers do not personally believe in civilizational or climate collapse, many of their series over the years have tapped into their viewers' archetypal fears. "The Last of Us" is no exception. Indeed, writers Neil Druckmann and Craig Mazin have deployed their skillful radar apparatus to penetrate deeply into the traumatized psyche of post-pandemic America.

Going forward, I will use the term *polycrisis,* rather than collapse, to describe the apocalyptic predicament in which humanity is currently embroiled. In 2022, the University of Bath in England defines the polycrisis in this way:

Over recent years we have experienced a period of significant global change. In addition to the acceleration of climate change, extreme weather events and environmental degradation, we are living through a global pandemic, a war in Europe, rising geopolitical tensions, high inflation and a cost of living crisis, energy supply and trade disruption, and widespread food insecurity.

These multiple and overlapping crises of our time mean we are now in the midst of a global polycrisis. These interconnected challenges aren't experienced by countries in isolation. Rather, they are problems of the global commons, and they cannot be solved by one country or group of countries.

You have probably picked up this book because the title and subtitle have attracted you, and they have probably attracted you because something in you resonates with the word *apocalypse*, and something else within you senses that you may need some tools in order to cope with even thinking about it, let alone experiencing it.

I do not know the ultimate consequences of the polycrisis, and I'm certain that it will continue to play out long after I have left the planet. I have no idea what horrors humans will experience because of it, nor do I know if future pandemics will turn people into the kinds of grotesque zombies depicted in *The Last of Us*. What I do know is that whatever the horrors, there will be moments, perhaps even years, when people will discover what Bill and Frank discover in the third episode of *The Last of Us*. Followed by the series' first two episodes of revulsion and trauma, two men fall in love and into their deepest, sweetest, most tender humanity while being surrounded by incalculable suffering. Just as no one prepared them for the monstrosity of the world around them, no one gave them a book of meditations and reflections on how to prepare emotionally and spiritually for it.

Part of us can fall into victim consciousness as the polycrisis deepens, and no doubt, part of you already has. We are all victims. And yet, we are all co-creators of our predicament. The mature adult, however, while acknowledging their victimization, also steps up to the plate and asks: *What do I do now with this situation? What is it asking of me? How can I be a death doula-midwife to a dying planet and the living beings dying with it? How can I fortify myself for what lies ahead and is already unfolding, and how can I love and care for those who lack little awareness of what the future holds?*

Not only is our planet dying, but it is dying in a particular way. Wealthy, mostly white males, have decided that engorging their bank accounts and stuffing their stomachs is the most ego-satiating reason for existence. The rest of us have bought into myriad versions of their delusion, but now the bills are coming due. In an effort to postpone the inevitable, many nations have chosen authoritarian leaders and policies that will soon consign most of the planet to totalitarianism. From there, it is only a short distance from rendering Earth largely uninhabitable for humans.

Even so, there will be "Bill's" and "Frank's" who experience more beauty, more meaning and more achingly gorgeous devotion to who and what matters most than they could have previously imagined—all in the midst of what may be the darkest hours in human history. This book is meant to provide humble points of light in what may become an endless night.

But why the title *Apocalypse Anytime?* While a collective, planetary apocalypse may occur over a duration of time, each of us experiences our own mini-apocalypses every day, sometimes many times a day. They are shorter and less protracted crises, but they confront us with our finite humanity, our vulnerability, and the reality that impermanence is the only constant in our lives. The intention of this book is to support the reader in navigating both the longer-term polycrisis and the daily impasses that challenge us on a smaller scale.

THREE COMMON PERSPECTIVES ON THE POLYCRISIS

While anyone who has even superficially engaged with the poly-crisis has some opinion about it, it is easy to notice three general perspectives.

Hell Fire and Brimstone. The first is an adamant "certainty" about when the consequences of the crises will come to fruition and an equally strident "certainty" about how it will unfold. These folks have usually remained largely cerebral in their engagement with it and have managed to avoid feeling it in any depth. Often, they are fixated on "collapse" and structure their activities, relationships, time, and planning around it. Frequently, they are reluctant to engage, not only with people who are not awake to the polycrisis, but specifically people who do not perceive it with the same dire level of urgency. Their attitude toward those who are "clueless" is one of arrogance and even hostility. Their predominant emotions in relation to the poly-crisis are fear and anger. They may be estranged from family members or friends who refuse to talk about collapse. At the same time, they may spend hours online reading or watching videos about the polycrisis, sign up for courses on the topic, or even travel long distances to participate in conferences featuring various experts on the topic. Sometimes they describe them-selves as "preppers" who have large supplies of food in their basements and who perhaps have firearms and ammunition on hand. They may have taken crisis or emergency response training to prepare for mass casualty events. They may resort to conspiracy theories about the polycrisis and about those who do not accept their version of it. They tend to avoid discussions of emotional or spiritual preparation for societal unraveling because they are highly focused on survival—or its opposite, suicide.

Collapse Acceptance—Sort of. These folks may have been aware of the polycrisis for years or even decades and may have spent some time being "hell fire and brimstoners." Often, they are meaningfully engaged with doing what they can to mitigate the damage of the polycrisis, such as growing robust organic gardens, living minimally and simplistically, living off-grid as much as possible, home schooling their children, creating polycrisis-aware communities and support systems in their region. They may have allowed themselves to feel deeply about a daunting future, including engaging in conscious grieving. However, in recent years they have come to "accept" collapse. But "acceptance" is a complicated word, particularly if the so-called "negative" emotions around the polycrisis are denied or suppressed in the name of acceptance. I have heard some people who claim to accept collapse declare that they no longer feel a need to grieve because they have fully accepted it. I have become wary of the word "acceptance" when speaking of collapse, because very subtly and seductively, "acceptance" can be a form of grief-suppression and attachment to feeling happy most of the time.

Acceptance of the polycrisis is tricky and often self-deceptive. None of us wishes to dwell constantly on a perilous future and the feelings that attend that likelihood. It is tempting to rely on Elizabeth Kubler-Ross's stages of grief model to endeavor to reach acceptance, but we do well to remember that she argued that people could reach some modicum of acceptance *because of*, not in spite of, their grief. As someone who has been thinking and feeling about the polycrisis for more than 15 years and who has more recently written extensively about experiencing joy in the midst of it, I do not wish to disparage collapse acceptance, but one key ingredient is and always will be essential.

Apocalypse Anytime. Below the reader will encounter a quote from Stephen Jenkinson, who states that from his perspective, *We are born to a dangerous time. Consider that an affliction or consider it an assignment.* At whatever stage of learning about and engaging with the polycrisis we may be, it is crucial that we remain students of it. We may now hold numerous metaphorical "degrees" in collapse preparation, but we must always be willing to bow in surrender to what it wants to teach us, not how we would prefer to feel.

It was also Jenkinson who suggested that grief never quite leaves the room, but is always a whisper in the room. Given our Western proclivity for linear thinking, it is easy to interpret Kubler-Ross's stages of grief as reaching an endpoint in which "the grieving part is over." She would have told us otherwise, and so have so many other grief sages since then. It is equally valid to assert that just as there are stages of grief, there are also stages of acceptance. Who can ever "accept" that their child died or that a leg was severed from their body by an IED in war? Who can ever "accept" a cancer diagnosis or a tragedy that causes the ability to create art or music to vanish?

No one wants to complete the journey that grief seeks to take us on. In fact, whether we are steeped in the "hellfire and brimstone" perspective or the Collapse Acceptance-sort of mindset, collapse itself can become an alluring escape from the inner and outer work it is calling us to commit to. I have known individuals who would rather mire themselves in collapse obsession rather than feel the feelings and body sensations that full polycrisis awareness demands of us. Who knew that the end of the world, like any other drama, could be so seductive and so successful in distracting us from our personal and collective healing?

The Apocalypse Anytime perspective is one that holds life and human emotions very lightly, knowing that nothing is permanent or final and that conscious grieving is the doorway to more joy, meaning, and aliveness than we could possibly imagine. It is a bone-marrow commitment to healing work on ourselves, the land, and our fellow Earth dwellers. Apocalypse Anytime is a perspective that understands that the polycrisis is a twenty-first century buzzword for a deep and profound emotional and spiritual initiation into the mysteries and the most life-altering layers of our humanity and that that initiation does not begin or end with the polycrisis and how we engage with it. Can we dare to imagine that our deepest Self originated long before the crisis and will not be extinguished by it? Paradoxically, as we mourn every loss, we become more of what is everlasting and eternal, and that is the only "acceptance" that matters.

In the first section of the book, the word *Hope* is redefined and reimagined. Few words in the English language have been so misunderstood or misused. What does hope actually mean in a time of planetary hospice and potential human extinction?

Realistically attending to the reimagination of hope, the inevitability of *Descent* is disclosed. But what does personal and collective descent mean, and why is it necessary?

What would seem the polar opposite of descent is *Joy,* to which the third section of the book is devoted. Joy and happiness are teased apart, and joy's inextricable connection with grief is celebrated.

A final section on *Caring* asks us to consider that in apocalyptic times, much of our lives may be devoted to caring and being cared for. Self-absorption will sink humans more diabolically into the quicksand of despair, but from our caring, the possibility of an entirely new culture of caring may arise.

In his 2020 book, *Healing Collective Trauma*, Thomas Hubl wrote that "the ultimate question regarding the darkness we see outside us is not whether it will consume our world but instead whether we can reframe our understanding of that darkness. How can we come to recognize the dark as a part of ourselves so we may integrate its lessons, and through them, be transformed? And how would such healing, on a collective scale, advance the care of the planet that is our home?"

This book is essentially a workbook. If you have no intention of doing the work, you will find it boring. Do not waste your time. If, however, you want to do more than just "learn new stuff," if you are ready to become a death doula-midwife for yourself and other beings, you may discover the true meaning of *apokalypsis*, the Greek word for "the unveiling." What can be seen when the veil is removed? My heart's desire is that *you* will be seen by yourself as never before, and that we all will see and be seen in ways that are now impossible to imagine, and that in the seeing, we will know unequivocally the gorgeous implications of our sacred humanity.

Carolyn Baker,
Boulder, Colorado, 2023

When a bridge endures internal stress fractures, no one notices until several of them connect—and then, the bridge collapses. The bridge of human decency has begun to collapse in America. Consider, as well, that in pottery, when a plate starts to show a network of cracks, it's known as crazing. This is caused by a mismatch between the clay body and the glaze, which creates stresses greater than the glaze is able to withstand. If the mismatch between what's inside and outside is great enough, the plate will break. Our society has been in a process of craze and collapse. We are experiencing stresses greater than the agreements of society can currently withstand and our social contracts are starting to break.[1]

—Mark Nepo, *Surviving Storms*

PART ONE: HOPE

Our global predicament is severe and at times feels overwhelming. Most humans do not fully comprehend or even approach its enormous ramifications. After all, is it not more tolerable to preoccupy ourselves with the daily routine of career, childcare, homemaking, shopping, traveling, hobbies, amusement, and creativity? The only way many can even begin to face reality is to deny its harshness by insisting that despite it, there is hope. Humans are not capable of enduring suffering without holding onto some sliver of hope. Yet from my perspective, Western culture has settled for a superficial, one-dimensional definition of the word. More substantially, the deepest layer of hope is related to meaning and purpose, and only as we excavate this layer can we savor authentic hope.

The more we cling to superficial notions of hope, the more authentic hope *eludes* us and magical thinking about hope *deludes* us. The two aspects of this thinking that are most psychologically and spiritually damaging are passivity and attachment to outcome. Passive hope demands nothing of us and assumes that someone or something out there will solve the problem without our participation in the process. Equally infantilizing is the notion that if we cling to passive hopefulness, the outcome will be favorable. Furthermore, if the outcome is not to our liking, then we must necessarily change our course of action and invest our hope in actions that will reward the ego with a sense of satisfaction and a job well done.

This section of the book explores the deeper layers of hope and challenges our cultural assumptions by offering a more mature definition of hope beyond end-result ego enhancement. As we savor a more nuanced approach to hope, we discover how vapid the terms "optimist" and "pessimist" have become.

❦ I ❦

WHAT IS HOPE?

Come, are you ready to set out?
—Cynthia Bourgeault, *Mystical Hope*

Modernity has superficially defined hope as something that parts seas and pulls rabbits out of hats. It is passive and exists outside us. Something, or someone in the external world will do something to prevent catastrophic climate chaos from obliterating planet Earth. Technology will save us. Nations will confer and reach a consensus on environmental practices that will spare us from cataclysm. What is more, being hopeful implies that the outcome of our hope will be positive, rewarding, and will allow us to stand back and say, "Well, it could have been worse."

Conversely, genuine hope requires human agency. It is about being fully present to our predicament—physically, emotionally, mentally, and spiritually. When we are fully present, we take a risk—a risk of feeling discomfort and disorientation. At the same time, this authentic hope allows us to feel more alive, more available, more awake than we have ever been.

In her extraordinary book, *Active Hope*, Joanna Macy writes:

3

Active Hope is waking up to the beauty of life
on whose behalf we can act.
We belong to this world.
The web of life is calling us forth at this time...
With Active Hope we realize that there are adven-
    tures in store,
strengths to discover, and comrades to link arms
    with.
A readiness to discover the size and strength of
    our hearts,
our quickness of mind, our steadiness of purpose,
our own authority, our love for life,
the liveliness of our curiosity,
the unsuspected deep well of patience and
    diligence,
the keenness of our senses, and our capacity to
    lead.
None of these can be discovered in an armchair or
    without risk.[1]

❧

Knowing this, as Cynthia Bourgeault asks in Mystical Hope,
are you ready to set out?

✿ 2 ✿
MYSTICAL HOPE

We are born to a dangerous time.
Consider that an affliction or consider it an assignment.

—Stephen Jenkinson[1]

What does the word *mystical* actually mean? It is related to the word *mystery* as well as *mystique, mystify,* and *mysterious.* Apparently, the root syllable, *myst,* originated from the Greek and referred to a person who was initiated into the sacred rites of ancient Greece. Mystical knowledge is not rational, linear, or left-brain. It incorporates right brain awareness and spiritual insight. It is metaphysical or beyond the scope of the purely physical.

Mystical hope does not focus on a positive outcome or even a positive feeling. Countless humans have been hopeful in horrific situations, even when they were feeling miserable. One is reminded of Viktor Frankl in Auschwitz and Nelson Mandela in a South African prison. In these situations, or any other, mystical hope is the capacity to find meaning and purpose, however small or seemingly insignificant, in one's experience. In other words, mystical hope is inextricably connected with one's inner world, not an external outcome.

Mystical hope is not so much a question about how things will turn out, but rather, how we will show up, no matter the outcome. *Mystical hope is a commitment to meeting life as an assignment to be completed rather than an obstacle to be removed.* Author and former hospice worker Stephen Jenkinson writes, "We are born to a dangerous time. Consider that an affliction or consider it an assignment." In other words, the "hope" is in our acceptance of the assignment, not in its results.

Authentic hope is willingly active and steps up to life's challenges as assignments and initiations into the sacred mysteries of human existence. Living from this perspective enables us to deploy active hope and make meaning in almost any situation.

We all possess the capacity for mystical hope. To enhance mystical hope, we must keep reminding ourselves that it is within us, not out there. We must also lean into it rather than into rational hope that constantly tells us how things should turn out. Another word for this in all traditions is *surrender*—a word that does not mean giving *up* but giving *over* our attachment to outcomes.

Consider that rational, ego-driven hope
is nothing less than arguing with reality,
and what it creates is not comfort and well-being,
but more suffering.

✵ 3 ✵
HOPE IS NOT OPTIMISM

Hope is definitely not the same thing as optimism.
Hope is not the conviction that something will turn out well,
but hope is the certainty that something makes sense,
regardless of how it turns out.[1]

—Vaclav Havel

W hen Havel spoke of something making sense, he was not speaking of intellectual reasoning. Like Viktor Frankl, he had been imprisoned, not once, but many times for speaking out on behalf of justice and humanism. Havel's definition of hope echoes Bourgeault's notion of mystical hope:

> Either we have hope within us or we don't; it is a dimension of the soul; it's not essentially dependent on some particular observation of the world or estimate of the situation. Hope is not prognostication. It is an orientation of the spirit, an orientation of the heart; it transcends the world that is immediately experienced, and is anchored somewhere beyond its horizons.[2]

What Havel is referring to indirectly is the spiritual source of hope which demands that we be fully present to the situation, take responsibility for our part in creating it, and both find and make meaning in the midst of our suffering.

We are not the source of mystical hope. It is within us—or perhaps, we are also within it. Our challenge is to allow ourselves to be channels of hope by accepting the assignment with which we are being presented and take action accordingly. The action we take must be guided by mystical hope, not optimism or our own personal sense of how things "should" turn out.

⊙⊱⊙

As you reflect on mystical hope,
what word or phrase resonates with or challenges you?
What sensations do you notice in your body?
What is yours to do?

❧ 4 ❧

ABANDON HOPE

Renunciation is a teaching to inspire us
to investigate what's happening every time
we grab something because we can't stand
to face what's coming.
—Pema Chodron[1]

B uddhism, among other traditions, does not glorify hope. In fact, many Buddhist teachers, including Pema Chodron, are fond of emphasizing that hope often feeds our denial and the illusion that we can avoid impermanence and the suffering that attends it. Echoing some of the other voices we have already heard on hope, Buddhist teachings offer practices for opening to the myriad forms of suffering we encounter in the way that Stephen Jenkinson has suggested—perceiving them as assignments that present us with opportunities to become wiser, kinder, and more compassionate human beings.

As we contemplate catastrophic climate change, for example, our challenge is to find meaning in the suffering that it entails. This is not to suggest that we do not work to mitigate climate catastrophe, but that as we do, we allow ourselves to be constantly confronted with the suffering and impermanence inherent in the destruction of the planet. In that suffering, we have the opportunity to open to mystical hope and the spiritual and emotional resources within that make meaning and inspire purpose. Yet more is required. Invariably attending our experience of mystical hope is the imperative of responding with action that serves other suffering beings.

When we find ourselves resorting to hope as a means of resisting the dread of present and future pain, we can, without shaming ourselves, be curious about our denial and feel compassion for ourselves and all who are suffering alongside us.

᛭

An appropriate reflection at this juncture might be:
What heartbreak does my hope temporarily insulate me from?
How might I compassionately alleviate the suffering
in another living being?

A DISHEARTENING DUO:
HOPE AND FEAR

And yet, such a wild ride between hope and fear is unavoidable. Fear is the necessary consequence of feeling hopeful again. Contrary to our belief that hope and fear are opposites where one trumps the other, they are a single package, bundled together as intimate, eternal partners. Hope never enters a room without fear at its side. If I hope to accomplish something, I'm also afraid I'll fail. You can't have one without the other.
—Margaret Wheatley, "The Place Beyond Hope and Fear"[1]

For Margaret Wheatley, hope is a setup. Passive hope provides a false sense of optimism and may move us into action, but as soon as we begin to act, we realize that we might fail, and we soon discover that we have traded the fear of the condition we want to feel hopeful about, for example, climate catastrophe, for the fear of not being able to eliminate or alleviate it.

I no longer believe that most of humanity can be spared from climate catastrophe and in fact, may be facing partial or near total extinction. The entire paradigm of industrial civilization is unraveling along with the belief systems on which the paradigm was founded. I have been asked how it feels to have "given up hope." My reply? It feels wonderful. Giving up hope releases me from fear, shame, and a sense of responsibility for fixing what is almost certainly unfixable.

However, in order to inhabit that spiritual and emotional space, I have had to accept the groundlessness that is inherent in the collapse of systems. Past human behavior has brought us to where we are now, and our future is perilously uncertain. Therefore, the only ground we have is the present moment. However, staying present is nearly impossible at times. We want to judge the past ("if only...) and cling to hope for the future, but as Wheatley reminds us, "All fear (and hope) arises from looking backward or forward. The present moment is the only place of clear seeing unclouded by hope or fear."

If we are pre-occupied with the past or the future, we are not able to be present, and being present is the only place where right action, meaningful action, action that makes a difference can occur.

❧

Suggested reflection: What is mine to do right now?

❦ 6 ❧

HOPE AND THE OPPRESSION
OF OUTCOME

Do not depend on the hope of results...you may have to face the fact that your work will be apparently worthless and even achieve no result at all, if not perhaps results opposite to what you expect. As you get used to this idea, you start more and more to concentrate not on the results, but on the value, the rightness, the truth of the work itself... You gradually struggle less and less for an idea and more and more for specific people... In the end, it is the reality of personal relationship that saves everything.
—Thomas Merton, *Letter to a Young Activist*[1]

Just as hope is a setup, so is attachment to the outcome of our actions in the world. The more attached we are, the more fearful of failure we become. Attachment to outcome leads to other emotions that are not useful. Anger, resentment, shame, and a toxic sense of responsibility may also distort our endeavors.

Attachment in any form minimizes our ability to be fully present to our predicament. In fact, what matters more than outcomes are the relationships we develop as we engage in our work. As Margaret Wheatley notes, "We are consoled and strengthened by being together. We don't need specific outcomes. We don't need hope. We need each other."[2]

Outcome oppression is a seduction by the ego to invest in what the ego can accomplish, not what might want to happen through us, in spite of, and beyond what the ego believes must happen.

What if the action we take does not bear fruit for another century, and we see little or no results in our lifetime? What if we are only planting seeds, and we will never bear witness to the harvest? Some would ask, "So what is the point?" The point is not results, but our commitment to doing the right thing because it is the right thing to do. The point is to do what we cannot *not* do.

Rarely in life do we have the privilege of witnessing the most profound results of our endeavors. As a former psychotherapist, I will never know the full extent to which I helped another person. As a former college professor, I will never know the exact number of students for whom my classes made a difference in their lives. I will never know how many became educators themselves and are now influencing other lives.

⚜

Suggested reflection:
What is it like not to know the outcome of my actions in the world?

❧ 7 ❧
HOPE IS THE ENEMY OF GRIEF

Grief requires us to know the time we're in. The great enemy of grief is hope. Hope is the four-letter word for people who are unwilling to know things for what they are. Our time requires us to be hope-free.[1]
—Stephen Jenkinson

The implication from Jenkinson is that if we are clutching onto our hope, we are deluded about the time we are living in. A world that may be annihilated by climate catastrophe, torn apart by human violence, and largely dominated by autocratic tyrants is not a world where passive hope that focuses on a "successful" outcome is appropriate or useful. Speaking as a long-time hospice worker, Jenkinson argues that our work is not to hope but to grieve, and ungrounded delusions that prevent us from being present to our grief are not allies but adversaries.

Grief sage Francis Weller, speaks of *ambient grief*—that is, the condition of our current era is comparable to marinating in loss on multiple levels twenty-four hours per day.

When I dialog with both those who cling to hope and those who cynically insist that the extinction of our species is inevitable, I encounter individuals who are grief-avoidant. They may genuinely believe that they are grieving the losses resulting from our predicament, but their adamant attachment to a specific outcome reveals their isolation from heartfelt sorrow. Mourning can only occur when we feel profoundly hopeless in the face of loss. Those who prognosticate that humans are guaranteeing their own extinction are ingesting a different kind of "hopium" whose name is "certainty." Both hope and certainty maintain a disembodied state of numbness that prevents us from immersing ourselves willingly into the searing emotions of loss.

Grief guarantees that both the optimism of hope and the rageful contempt for a species making itself extinct will be undermined by the gut-wrenching sorrow of recognizing a planet on life-support in which millions of living beings are dying daily even as our hearts break with helplessness to alter the likely outcome. Moreover, this particular grief not only produces in us the sob of potential annihilation, but a lifetime of stifled sobs resulting from our socialization into a soul-murdering but "hopeful" culture.

And so I plead with us to abandon hope and to abdicate cynicism. The warm and healing waters of grief are too delicious to resist.

☙❧

What is your grief or griefs, and where do they live in your body?

JOURNAL PROMPTS ON HOPE

Not everyone likes to write in a journal, but journaling can be enormously illuminating by providing a space to reflect on one's past experiences, present-time challenges, and future unknowns. I recommend journaling for this purpose and as a gentle pathway to opening the door of the psyche to unconscious contents that may assist the healing process and that by coming to awareness, could support us in navigating personal and collective apocalypses.

The first section of this book focuses on hope and seeks to question how hope has been sold to us as some magic pill that makes the demise of our planet "all better."

To glean maximum benefit from reading this section of the book and in order to redefine our relationship with hope, the following journaling questions may be useful:

- As you read this section of the book, what was most disturbing?
- What was validating or reassuring?
- How has "having hope" served you in the past?
- How has "being hopeful" failed you in the past?

- How would you like to engage with hope going forward?

PART TWO: DESCENT

All mythology and indigenous wisdom from time immemorial has emphasized the necessity of descent into deeper layers of the human psyche in order to acquire greater wisdom for living wisely and compassionately in the world. In the late-nineteenth century, psychologist Carl Jung integrated this reality into his theories of soul healing. His experiences of working with patients reinforced his belief that in order to restore wholeness to the wounded psyche, we must consciously and willingly descend into the wound. Great skill, along with extensive support from others, is necessary, but if an individual understands the value of descent and is willing to descend, enormous healing and restoration are possible, and the pain of the descent is tempered by becoming conscious of it.

Mythologist and storyteller Michael Meade states that "the point of each experience of descent is to return to life as a greater soul with a clearer sense of purpose and a greater knowledge of how to serve the world at this time of radical change."[1] Meade also says, "Wisdom can reveal the light hidden in dark times; but it requires that we face the darkness in ourselves.

People may desire pearls of wisdom, yet most are unwilling to descend to the depths where the pearls wait to be found. Wisdom involves a necessary descent into the depths of life, for that alone can produce 'lived knowledge' and a unified vision."[2]

Whether in the life of an individual or a culture, distressing times require descent to make sense of the adversity and utilize it on behalf of health and wholeness. The apocalypse in which we currently find ourselves as a species, as well as the apocalypses of our individual lives, require us to descend into them in order to heal from them and carry that healing into our lives and our world. This journey of descent is more than figuring out our "causes and cures" and compels us to open to the emotions inherent in the pain. In this way, not only is healing possible, but by descending, we can discern the appropriate actions to take in response.

Both those who cling to passive hope and those who are engulfed in pessimism and despair are uninformed by descent because they have not consciously engaged with it. A hopeful person is unlikely to descend into the pain, and the despairing person may appear to be making a descent into the pain while actually avoiding it by refusing to enter the waters of grief.

Ultimately, a descent willingly accepted and engaged with results in an ascent—a return to one's pre-descent life, but now more fully informed and illumined by the experience of descent. Return from the descent brings not only deeper wisdom, but clarity on what actions to take going forward. As we will see, the journey of descent provides a greater capacity to fully savor authentic joy and to meet our crumbling world with extraordinary compassion.

❦ 8 ❦

DOORWAYS INTO DESCENT

One cannot pursue happiness; if he does, he obscures it. If he will proceed with the human task of life, the relocation of the center of gravity of the personality to something greater outside itself, happiness will be the outcome. [1]

—Robert Johnson, Jungian analyst

I n Greek mythology, the young goddess Persephone was fond of picking flowers in the meadow. One day, as she was happily engaged in acquiring a large bouquet of them, the other gods caused the earth to split under her feet, and she slipped beneath the ground into the underworld where Hades, the god of the underworld, trapped and married her. Although Persephone hated the underworld and Hades at first, she came to love and live happily with him.

In our human experience, we have all had Persephone moments—moments of simply living our lives and doing what we love, only to be suddenly and tragically plunged into the underworld darkness of catastrophe, loss, and heartbreak. In an instant, we find ourselves in a living hell (a word synonymous with Hades), and we abhor what is happening to us. Sometimes we adapt and make the best of the tragedy, but often we don't—

our descent into the underworld is never fully acknowledged, or the pain of the calamity is anesthetized with substances, romance, extreme busyness, and an incessant flurry of activity and avoidance. In such instances, we do not recognize the descent as such, nor do we come to understand its meaning or purpose in our lives or even the reality that such purpose exists.

In the same way that individual humans experience descents, so do nations, cultures, communities, and families. Just as Stephen Jenkinson asks us to respond to descents as "assignments," it is our task as sentient beings to ask the proper questions regarding our time in the underworld. How did I get here? What work needs to be done in order to ascend from Hades with a transformed vision of my identity and purpose?

Persephone was swept into the underworld while pursuing her own happiness. She learned to live there. Perhaps she eventually discovered the meaning of her unwanted descent, but we do not know that with certainty. What we do know is that *we* can question the meaning and purpose of our own and humanity's descent.

❧

What purposes are you discovering in our collective descent?

❦ 9 ❦

LIFE-ALTERING DESCENT

*No one should deny the danger of the descent, but it can be risked. No one
need risk it, but it is certain that someone will. And let those who go
down the sunset way do so with open eyes, for it is a sacrifice which
daunts even the gods. Yet every descent is followed by an ascent; the
vanishing shapes are shaped anew, and a truth is valid in the end only if
it suffers change and bears new witness in new images, in new tongues,
like a new wine that is put into new bottles.*
—Carl Jung, *Symbols of Transformation*

For a moment the reader may believe that Jung is saying
we have a choice to make the descent or not—that like
a subscription to a streaming service, we can sign up
and cancel whenever we like. In fact, no one ever has a choice to
sign up for a descent. Like Persephone, we can only realize that
we have been abducted to a form of hell and be open to how the
descent may want to instruct us. If we do consent, Jung says we
must do so with open eyes.

The point, he says, is transformation. Not "change." Not self-
improvement. Not some new paint and wallpaper in the
ramshackle rooms of the psyche that we have disowned or never
realized were there. What is happening to humankind at this

moment is a massive descent into unprecedented darkness and suffering. While there is much that we can do to temper the severity of the demise, it will be dangerous and "daunts even the gods."

But ascent is inevitable—not necessarily a one-time blowout extravaganza of homecoming from the battle, but moments *within* the psychological and spiritual conflagration that reassure us that our unwanted companionship with Hades matters—that our suffering means something for ourselves and possibly for those who suffer with us.

Many humans do and will experience our collective demise as a kind of victimization by the gods—those "others" who created a mess that one believes one was "too smart" to create. They refuse to own their part and so view it as an affliction, not an assignment.

☙❧

The collective descent has already begun.
As you personally descend, what do you fear?
What support will you need,
and what support can you give others?

❧ 10 ❧

THE INESCAPABLE SHADOW

*Everything with substance casts a shadow. The Ego stands to the shadow
as light to shade. This is the quality that makes us human. Much as we
would like to deny it, we are imperfect. And perhaps it is in what we
don't accept about ourselves—our aggression and shame, our guilt and
pain—that we discover our humanity.*
—*Meeting the Shadow*, Connie Zweig, Jeremiah Abrams[1]

Although Sigmund Freud wrote extensively about the
dark side of humanity, Carl Jung identified a walled-off
part of the human psyche where we put the defective
parts of us, the parts we are ashamed of. He called it the shadow.
The shadow consists essentially of those aspects of ourselves
that we send away or disown because they are not acceptable to
us or to others. Most humans go to extraordinary lengths to
deny and conceal the shadow, yet it invariably makes its presence
known—if not to ourselves, then to others in the course of our
relationships with them. One way this happens is through
projection—attributing to another person or group something
we find unacceptable in ourselves.

Whenever a person or culture experiences a descent, the
shadow is invariably encountered. The knee-jerk reaction of

most is to project it onto someone or something else. However, when we understand what the shadow is and that we all have one, we may gradually begin to recognize it as such before disowning or projecting it—an awareness that can minimize the further decimation of our planet and the harm we cause it, ourselves, and each other.

In a time of cultural descent, unacknowledged shadows explode everywhere, and while we cannot prevent or stop that from happening, we can be attuned to our own shadow so that we do less harm and more skillfully respond to our own shadow behavior and that of others.

As we make external preparations for a collapsing society, we can minimize our personal collapses by doing conscious shadow work. My book *Dark Gold: The Human Shadow and the Global Crisis* provides specific tools for doing that work, but other practices are being offered in this book.

❧

A starting point may simply be to ask the question:
What do I know about my shadow?
What do I dislike about it?

❧ II ❧
DARK SHADOW, BRIGHT SHADOW

The shadow is ninety-percent pure gold.
—Carl Jung[1]

This statement by Jung has at least two meanings. One meaning is that the shadow is not entirely comprised of darkness. Jung sometimes spoke of the "golden shadow," by which he meant positive qualities that we disown alongside the negative. If we disown qualities that we believe are unsafe to express, whether positive or negative, those qualities become part of the shadow. For example, a small boy growing up in a family where anger by males is permitted, but crying and tenderness are not, quickly learns to disown the latter qualities in order to be accepted by his family. Anger and tenderness become part of his shadow. A little girl may learn early-on that females in her family are not permitted to express anger, and so she disowns her anger, which becomes part of her shadow.

If the man who was formerly that young boy can access his sorrow and gentleness which lie buried in his shadow, those disowned qualities can become "pure gold" for him. Likewise, if the grown woman who sent away her anger in childhood can access it as an adult and claim it as acceptable and empowering for herself, she has discovered the gold in her shadow, which we sometimes call the "bright" shadow, as opposed to the "dark" shadow.

The second possible meaning of Jung's statement, "the shadow is ninety-percent pure gold," is that as we do the inner work of befriending the shadow, we invariably experience more wholeness. Whenever any part of us is disowned, we become psychologically fragmented, but reclaiming what we have disowned heals the brokenness, and in that healing lies the gold. Moreover, Jung pointed out that it takes enormous energy to continue repressing the shadow, but when we consciously work with the shadow, much of that energy naturally spawns our untapped creativity and passion for life.

Making peace with the shadow is often a painful, unwelcome process, yet most individuals discover that in doing so, the parts of themselves that they have disowned, perhaps so long ago that they barely remember disowning them, become for them "pure gold."

❦

Do you recall disowning, hiding, rejecting, sending away parts of yourself that were not acceptable to others?

❧ 12 ❧

101 WAYS TO BYPASS THE SHADOW

What spiritual bypassing would have us rise above is precisely what we need to enter, and enter deeply, with as little self-numbing as possible. To this end, it is crucial that we see through whatever practices we have, spiritual or otherwise, that tranquilize rather than illuminate and awaken us.

—Robert Augustus Masters[1]

In a world as stressed, overworked, underpaid, traumatized, anxious, violent, and despairing as ours, most people have no understanding of the shadow and wish to avoid the topic at all costs. Western culture in particular has infantilized us to pursue instant gratification, material rewards, ego inflation, and psychic numbing as exquisite forms of avoidance of the shadow.

Circumventing shadow work assumes many forms, including the use of religion and spirituality. All spiritual traditions have some awareness of evil and humanity's capacity for being ensnared by it. Yet many forms of spirituality lack awareness of the shadow as Jung described it and offer teachings and techniques which avoid or claim to soothe or minimize difficult emotions such as sorrow, anger, fear, and anxiety. They may encourage us to forget our personal histories and live only in the now. They aspire to transcend the human condition and focus only on positive emotions and outcomes.

Cultures and nations bypass their shadows by emphasizing patriotism, democratic ideals, heroism, and positive past behavior to minimize or deny their shadows. For example, United States history minimizes the consequences of bringing millions of people of color, against their will, to its shores. It falsely justifies its involvement in numerous wars of conquest and acquisition in the name of "progress." America stole millions of acres of land from native peoples and pillaged and polluted water, land, and air on behalf of corporate capitalism. Not only has the United States never fully acknowledged the role of the shadow in its history, but according to some, even teaching the dark side of its history is "unpatriotic" and would cause children to feel uncomfortable with it or responsible for events that happened generations before they were even born.

Our propensity for bypassing the shadow is endless and nearly effortless. Yet shadow healing happens *in* descent, not in "rising above."

⁂

How are you drawn to "rise above" or deny your shadow?

❧ 13 ❧
THE CULT OF INNOCENCE

I don't trust a spirituality that doesn't have dirt under its fingernails.
—Brené Brown[1]

Many ancient and indigenous traditions recognize and incorporate the shadow into their rituals and practices. For example, the Hopi tradition includes clown characters who portray the shadow in public rituals and dances. Often, their behavior is rude and obnoxious during the ritual, but it is a teaching moment for the community. It's as if they are saying, "Watch us closely, because we are acting out what all humans do—including you."

Christianity, on the other hand, has traditionally disowned the shadow and attacked it. It often did this through conquest and colonialization, claiming that its converts, usually people of color, needed to be "saved" from sin. This "othering" of people who were not Christians created a cult of innocence and superiority. In fact, because the colonizing Christian was "innocent," they were "superior," but upon reflection, claiming superiority because of one's innocence is anything but innocent.

More recently, Christian pastors and theologians such as Nadia-Bolz Weber, Richard Rohr, Brian McClaren, Jacqui Lewis, and Anthea Butler are passionately challenging the cult of innocence. Having wrestled with the shadow in their own lives and having witnessed its devastation in the lives of people in their care, they are pushing back against the cult of innocence in the Christian tradition.

The cult of innocence manifests not only in Christianity but in nationalism and white privilege, homophobia, and misogyny. Spiritual bypassing of any kind is also a form of "othering" in that it assumes that one must maintain a positive attitude on the spiritual path and avoid negativity or adversity. "Negativity" is the "undesirable other," but positive thinking is "superior" and "innocent."

As individuals and communities descend in times of loss and collapse, we have the option of othering and defending our innocence, or recognizing the shadow in ourselves and in our world. Therefore, any spiritual path we might embrace must have dirt under its fingernails—starting with our own.

❧ 14 ❧
WHAT SHADOW HEALING
LOOKS LIKE

Our shadows hold the essence of who we are. They hold our most treasured gifts. By facing these aspects of ourselves, we become free to experience our glorious totality: the good and the bad, the dark and the light.
—Debbie Ford, *The Dark Side of the Light Chasers*[1]

As we consider the shadow in the context of the descent that individuals and nations are now experiencing as systems collapse, it is important to have a sense of shadow work and our own agency in doing it. Because everyone's shadow is different, everyone's shadow healing process will be different.

One aspect of the shadow that humans doing shadow work consistently feel is shame. As we become willing to explore the shadow, we often feel ashamed of what we see. However, shame itself is an aspect of the shadow, and becoming engulfed in shame is not useful. Instead, we must be able to detach from the shadow enough to view it with compassion and understand that it formed within us as a result of forces outside of us. Wounded people create other wounded people.

As a result of disowning parts of ourselves that were unacceptable to others, our shadow developed its toxicity and self-destructive impulses. While these are unpleasant to observe, it is important that we do. One of the most important qualities in doing shadow work is curiosity. Rather than judging what we see, we become curious about it which opens space to ask the questions we need to ask: What influenced me to become judgmental, self-critical, hostile, self-centered, self-destructive, dishonest, cowardly, people-pleasing, resentful, or any other qualities we discover in the shadow?

Curiosity then leads us to consciously observing the shadow by using techniques such as journaling, psychotherapy, body work, dream work, visualization, and more. We can also discuss shadow work with others who are doing that work and who will support us in the work rather than trying to make us feel better about ourselves.

In my book *Dark Gold*, I repeatedly emphasized the emotional and spiritual treasures that we can discover in working with the shadow. Not only might we discover our "bright" shadow, but we may experience an increase in previously unknown energy and creativity as we make the unconscious shadow conscious.

❧

What gifts do you imagine lie in your shadow?

JOURNAL PROMPTS ON THE SHADOW

- At this point you may be feeling a bit overwhelmed by the topic of the shadow. Perhaps you are feeling scared or simply discouraged by the enormity of the topic. Whatever you are feeling at this point, take time to write about it in your journal.
- When we explore the shadow, we invariably feel some shame as the topic becomes personal and concrete. What shame in you gets stirred as you consider your personal shadow? Does another part of you feel compassion for yourself and why you originally disowned certain parts of you?
- What do you know about your bright shadow? Where is the gold, and how might you "polish" it and express it in the world?

❧ 15 ❧

DESCENT = GRIEF

What we encounter, recognize, or discover, depends on the quality of our approach. An approach of reverence invites revelation. To pause and reflect on this can make all the difference between living in a cold, detached world, populated primarily by judgments and cynicism, and living in a world riddled with intimacy and offers of communion. When our approach is one of reverence, we find ourselves falling into a deeper embrace with all that is open to encounter, both internally and in the surrounding, breathing world.
—Francis Weller, "The Reverence of Approach"[1]

Inevitably, when we are in the throes of a descent, grief occupies much of the terrain. A descent compels us to feel the losses of our lives, past and present. Our fear of grief due to cultural messages and past experiences of shaming in relation to our sorrow cause us to stifle, suppress, and avoid grief at any cost.

Weller is gently reminding us that grief is something to be approached reverently, with respect and even awe. It is a natural, biological response to loss—any loss, and when we have adequate support for feeling our grief and are not alone with it, it almost always becomes a powerful healing force. Grief is a mystery. We do not know exactly how it works, but countless humans have discovered that when they reverence and cherish it, it pours out its mysterious gifts and makes them whole.

We have all been taught not to trust grief because it is a nuisance at best and an emotional vampire at worst. Yet Weller invites us to welcome the "homeless dog" with a reverence that opens to the possibility that grief comes bearing previously unrecognized gifts.

How radically different our culture might be if we were able to trust grief and deeply mourn what we have destroyed and what we have become. It is highly unlikely that collective grieving will occur on a large scale, but each individual has the opportunity to join with another individual or several to support and be supported in trusting the grieving process by reverently approaching it.

ॐ

What gifts might grief carry for you?

❧ 16 ❧

OUR DEFINITION OF GRIEF IS
TOO SMALL

Grief and love are sisters, woven together from the beginning.
Their kinship reminds us that there is no love
that does not contain loss and no loss
that is not a reminder of the love we carry
for what we once held close.
—Francis Weller, *The Wild Edge of Sorrow*

The majority of books written about grief are focused primarily on the death of a loved one or a pet. Someone whom I consider a grief sage, Francis Weller, has expanded our perspective and teaches his readers and audiences the Five Gates of Grief. These are:

- The First Gate: Everything We Love, We will Lose
- The Second Gate: The Places That Have Not
  Known Love
- The Third Gate: The Sorrows of the World
- The Fourth Gate: What We Expected and Did Not
  Receive
- The Fifth Gate: Ancestral Grief

When we expand our definition of grief, we understand how encompassing it is and how the threads of grief touch every aspect of our lives. Our work then, is to weave those threads into a cloth that is large and generous enough to enfold us, yet also allows the joy that lies at our core to comfort and inspire us.

Grief is symbolically a water element, as evidenced by our tears. Grief asks us to allow its waters to flow freely, and like a river, it will eventually find its own place in our psyche and in our relationships. When it is "dammed" or repressed by us out of fear that we will become inundated with its waters, the natural flow of grief is blocked, leading to depression which, in the language of Francis Weller, is unmetabolized grief.

In traditional and indigenous cultures, grief is not a private issue. Everyone in the community participates in everyone else's grief. Because grief has become a "private" matter in Western culture, we have come to believe that we must carry it alone, which causes us to fear it even more. For this reason, grieving alongside the support of others who respect and honor our grief is crucial.

۞

Which gate of grief is most alive for you in this moment?
You may want to read about the Five Gates
in detail (below) before answering this question.

Who might be your allies as you grieve?

❧ 17 ❧

EVERYONE WE LOVE, WE
WILL LOSE

Everything you love is very likely to be lost, but in the end, love will return in a different way.
—Franz Kafka[1]

Although Kafka insists that what we love will return to us in some form, this is likely to offer little comfort in a time of loss. When we lose a loved one, a beloved pet, our health, a dream, an opportunity, a human relationship, a job, a home—whatever the loss may be, we may hear Kafka's words, but we may not be able to take them in.

In the Buddhist tradition, impermanence is a fact of the human condition of which we are daily reminded in some fashion. Perhaps the last thing we could have imagined losing is our planet, and yet that is unfolding rapidly even as I write and you read these words. The Third Gate of grief is never far away.

Our challenge is not only to hold everything and everyone with the awareness that we will lose them, but to ponder our relationship with them. What does that person or that thing mean to us? What is their significance in our life? What difference have they made? Will we remember them fondly because we are stronger, kinder, wiser, more compassionate because of them? Or might we want to forget them because of the suffering they engendered in our lives? Will their departure fill us with gratitude for their presence in our lives, or will it encumber us with unfinished business, words we wish we had spoken, wounds that could never have been healed, mysteries that can never be solved, and regrets about what might have been?

Recently, Francis Weller has begun using the term "ambient grief," suggesting that loss is everywhere present in our world. It is as if we are marinating in grief with no escape, no respite from the sorrow of endings. Even as we attempt to cope with personal endings, the ubiquity of collective and community losses is staggering. Resistance to grieving becomes evermore futile and foolish and disempowering as the losses accumulate exponentially.

࿇

Take some time to contemplate the word "impermanence."
Reflect on the fact that we are constantly losing
people and things that we love, and that some day,
other beings who love us will also lose us.

❦ 18 ❦

THE PLACES THAT HAVE NOT
KNOWN LOVE

Shame is that warm feeling that washes over us, making us feel small,
flawed, and never good enough.
—Brené Brown[1]

Everyone in Western culture has been shamed. We have
been emotionally forced to send into our unconscious
the parts of us that were not welcomed by our family
or our culture. Rather than become total outcasts, we cast these
aspects out of ourselves and the rest of the world.

For centuries in Western culture, it has been shameful for
any boy to long to experience what it might be like to be a girl.
To act like a girl was to be called a "sissie." Girls who wanted to
feel like boys were not free to articulate their desire, but when
they were acting like boys, they were often labeled a "tomboy."

Imagine a boy who quite naturally felt tenderness and
empathy for a suffering animal or for his mother as she was
getting battered by his father. This boy was compelled to conceal
his pain and grief. After decades of hiding his sorrow under a
façade of anger, he attends a men's group where he has permission to cry and mourn. He suddenly bursts into tears.

A woman who has spent a lifetime repressing her anger and

focusing on "being nice" becomes enraged with her boss and throws a tantrum at the office, breaking coffee cups in the break room (you know, "break," but not coffee cups), followed by cursing, stomping out of the office, and screaming "I quit."

The tears erupting from the man and the tantrum erupting from the woman are parts of themselves that they have exiled for most of their lives. Those parts never knew love. But regardless of how painstakingly and successfully they were repressed, the outcast aspects eventually exploded because they were authentically human and could no longer be silenced.

The young boy who feared being called a sissie because he sometimes felt like a girl and the young girl who was labeled a tomboy may find themselves in the second decade of the twenty-first century, declaring that they are gay or lesbian or nonbinary or transgender or simply queer—or not. But at last, with myriad challenges, they are finally able to own all that they disowned early in life in order to survive.

ॐ

*What outcast parts of yourself did you have to disown
because they were not welcomed, loved, respected, or honored?*

What would it be like for you to own those "outcasts" today?

❧ 19 ❧

THE SORROWS OF THE WORLD

Follow the heartbreak.
—Andrew Harvey, *The Hope: A Guide to Sacred Activism*[1]

Humanity is engulfed in ecological devastation unprecedented in the modern world. Our habitat is dying, and our species, like so many that have already gone extinct, faces a similar future. What is more, the carrying capacity of our planet is far less than what we have foisted upon it, and phantom carrying capacity has fooled us into thinking that the Earth can support more of us than, in fact, it will be able to support in the future.

As the planet continues to wither, and as human behavior becomes more deranged as a result of our disconnection with ourselves, with each other, and the Earth, we are all soaking in ambient grief. Our behavior gives testimony to our despair through proliferating violence and suicide, our creating and refusing to resolve homelessness, our abuse of children and animals, aging populations afflicted with cognitive decline, and the prevalence of attention disorders among children.

What if our culture and the Earth itself *needs* our grief? What if, through our willingness to consciously grieve our planetary predicament, we might become more intimately engaged with the entire web of life and all living beings? Technology, conferences on climate change, civil disobedience, and tree planting cannot nurture this love affair. Grieving can.

Why should we follow the heartbreak? Because heartbreak catapults us into grief, and grief magnetically draws us into service. As we have seen, our service is not about outcome or results. It is about restoring *us* to wholeness as much as those we serve. Just as our work in the world is simply the right thing to do, grieving is unequivocally the right thing to do.

Likewise, grieving carries us to remorse—recognizing our part, whatever it has been, in creating the horrors we now mourn. The sorrows of the world scream to us that grief is no longer a private affair and never has been. Grief has the potential to remake us from the inside out—to produce a new species of humanity.

◌⁂◌

In the labyrinth of the sorrows of the world,
what is your heartbreak?

What action might result if you follow it into service?

WHAT WE EXPECTED BUT DID NOT RECEIVE

*It may sound surprising when I say, on the basis of
my own clinical practice as well as that of my
psychological and psychiatric colleagues,
that the chief problem of people in the
middle decade of the twentieth century
is emptiness.*
—Rollo May[1]

Although 70 years have passed since Rollo May wrote these words, the blight of emptiness continues to afflict the human condition, particularly in Western culture. In his research on archetypes or universal themes in the human experience, Carl Jung asserted that humans are wired for many of the guiding principles that we find in ancient, traditional societies such as ritual, extended family, rites of passage, community grieving, and the integration of the natural world into daily life.

The Fourth Gate of Grief is the sorrow within us regarding people, things, activities, and traditions that we expected but did not receive. Writing about the Fourth Gate, Erin Geesman Rabke states that:

It's as if we were wired for the whole human experience that our deep time ancestors knew by heart, through experience.[2]

They would gather to share rituals of grief and gratitude. They would sing together. They would share meals together. They would share dreams. They would hunt together. They would gather food and firewood. They would tell stories at night. They knew the myths; they knew the intimacies of the land base that they were on. This is what shaped us over millions of years and most precisely in the last 300,000 years when we became homo sapiens.

And now in the blink of an eye, we've abandoned almost every one of those coordinates. So we feel lost and empty in this world. We lack a sense of place and direction and belonging. But it's still wired inside of us.

The tragedy is we end up blaming ourselves for this feeling of emptiness. "What did I do wrong that I feel so empty?" Well, what if this emptiness isn't a defect on my part, but rather the failure of a culture that can no longer materialize the things that humans require to stay healthy and alive and exuberant?

۞

What are some ways you could help bring back the old rituals, in your family and in your community?

✳ 21 ✳

ANCESTRAL GRIEF

It is this power of ancestors that will help us direct our lives and avoid falling into huge ditches. Ancestor spirits can see the future, past, and present. They can see inside us and outside of us.
—Sobonfu Somé, late elder of the Dagara Tribe, Burkina Faso[1]

A growing body of research suggests that trauma (for example, from childhood abuse, family violence, or food insecurity, among many other things) can be passed from one generation to the next. Trauma can leave a chemical mark on a person's genes, which can then be passed down to future generations. This mark doesn't cause a genetic mutation, but it does alter the mechanism by which the gene is expressed. This alteration is not genetic, but *epigenetic.* [2]

Western psychological research is beginning to discover what indigenous societies have known for centuries, namely, that our interactions with ancestors leaves its mark on us in myriad ways. We are influenced by the experiences of our ancestors, even if we never met them. Nearly all Jewish children have ancestral memory of the holocaust. Native American children have ancestral memory of European invaders. Even if one argues that ancestral memory does not exist, and individuals are influenced by what they have been *told* about their ancestors, modern research is beginning to reveal that even without any information about ancestors, we are still influenced by them.

Indigenous cultures understand that we carry the wounds of our ancestors, even if we never met them. Those cultures also know that our ancestors who are no longer with us can support us in the grieving/healing process. Might grieving for our ancestors not only facilitate their healing, but ours as well?

☙❧

What do you know about the grief of your ancestors?

What grief of theirs might you be carrying?

*Have you considered talking to them,
even if you feel foolish and skeptical in doing so?*

If so, what would you say or ask for?

DESCENT DOES NOT EQUAL
DEPRESSION

*When people arrive at my office, typically the complaint is one of
depression. When I sit with them for any length of time, it becomes
apparent that what they're suffering from isn't so much depression but
oppression. They are weighted down by the unmetabolized sorrows of a
lifetime. Not being able to identify them as grief, as losses, it's hard to
really mourn them.*
—Francis Weller[1]

W hen the topic of grief surfaces in my interactions
with clients and acquaintances, people often
express concern that if they engage with their grief
"too much," they may become depressed. Weller's distinction
above is invaluable in distinguishing the difference between the
two. Grief allows us to mourn specific losses rather than
compress them into the shadow where, unmetabolized, they
become depression.

Often attending our fear of "depression" around grieving is
the extremely oppressive deterrent of shame. When grief begins
to bubble up in the soul, we not only fear a psychological condition, but the cultural messages we receive about grief begin
shaming us for not being able to "tough it out" and be strong.

Shame argues that others have it worse or that our grandfather suffered through the Great Depression or World War II or both and that we should put on our big boy or girl pants and persevere. After all, says shame, you are not a homeless refugee in Syria or Ukraine. Be thankful that you are even alive.

Much of what is diagnosed as depression is frequently unmetabolized grief—grief that has nowhere to go when its naturally tearful waters become frozen. Conscious grieving for our losses begins the process of melting rivers of tears, releasing and restoring the natural flow of the waters of grief.

To be human is to mourn. From the losses resulting from the small, daily apocalypses of our lives to the incalculable losses of our collective planetary apocalypse, our souls cry out to name them and grieve them. Fear and shame protest this naked, natural response to loss which is why we need the support of allies to have our backs as we protest our familial and cultural programming with our tears.

Only in Western civilization has grief ever been a private matter. Ancient and traditional cultures have always understood the healing power of collective grief.

❦

Who are your allies as you consciously enter the waters of grief?

GRIEF IS DOING ITS WORK
IN YOU

*So you must not be frightened if a sadness rises up before you, larger than
any you have ever seen; if a restiveness, like light and cloud shadows,
passes over your hands and over all you do. You must think that
something is happening with you, that life has not forgotten you, that it
holds you in its hand; it will not let you fall. Why do you want to shut out
of your life any uneasiness, any miseries, or any depressions? For after all,
you do not know what work these conditions are doing inside you.*
Rainer Maria Rilke, *Letters to a Young Poet*[1]

*Every transformation demands as its precondition 'the ending of a
world'—the collapse of an old philosophy of life.*
—Carl Jung, *Man and His Symbols*[2]

We can trust conscious grief work because it changes
us. Medical and psychological research reveals
enormous physical and emotional benefits when
people allow themselves to grieve consciously.

I know from the experiences of people who are committed
to grief work that it has a profound effect on how those individuals relate to themselves and the world around them. Many
people report that allowing themselves to grieve deeply has

refined their capacity to feel joy. Almost without exception, people report feeling more alive and embodied. Increased feelings of compassion and empathy are a common result of conscious grief work, as is the experience of feeling grounded and more at peace with oneself and other sentient beings. When we are determined to eliminate discomfort from our lives, we also eliminate the opportunity that grieving offers us to experience these outcomes.

In late 1902, a 19-year-old officer cadet in the Theresian Military Academy in Austria was reading the poetry of Rainer Maria Rilke. To his surprise, he found out that Rilke himself used to attend military education, but did not complete it. The young cadet was himself conflicted between pursuing a career in writing or a career in the military. He thought he would write to Rilke and ask him to critique his poetry and ask for advice with his dilemma. In February, 1903, he received a reply. Their correspondence quickly moved past critiquing poetry, continuing back and forth until 1908. A few years after Rilke's death in 1926, his correspondent, Franz Xaver Kappus, compiled and published 10 of his letters with Rilke in a collection called *Letters to a Young Poet*.

In any time of "apocalypse," we will suffer regardless of how we respond to it, but from Rilke's perspective, times of suffering are golden opportunities to be transformed by pain. "Do not squander the hour of your pain," he wrote, "don't waste your suffering."[3]

Talking to grief works upon it—changes it. And embracing our grief changes us.

꧁꧂

What "work" has conscious grieving done in you?

❧ 24 ❧

A CULTURE IN DESCENT

Ecological understanding of the human predicament indicates that we live in times when the American habit of responding to a problem by asking "All right, now what do we do about it?" must be replaced by a different query that does not assume all problems are soluble: "What must we avoid doing to keep from making a bad situation unnecessarily worse?"
—William Catton, Jr., *Overshoot: The Ecological Basis of Revolutionary Change*[1]

It would be more than enough for any of us to contain if the only demise to which we were asked to surrender was exclusively individual. Yet concurrently, Western culture is in unprecedented decline. William Catton asserts that we have exceeded the carrying capacity of our planet, which invariably results in the dissolution of societies and the massive extinction of species. He asserts that the collapse of industrial civilization and the misery that attends it is a *fait accompli.* Asking "What can we do about it?" is like asking if repainting the cars involved in a fatal crash will bring the victims back to life.

While we cannot prevent or reverse the collapse, we can commit our lives to minimizing the emotional and spiritual damage this collective descent will activate. While our thoughts may immediately leap to massive efforts on a large scale, one way we can alleviate suffering is by grieving—consciously, intentionally, and with each other's support.

Grieving together accelerates empathy, compassion, and solidarity in our suffering. It minimizes a false sense of hope and enlivens us with a vibrant sense of meaning and purpose. What is more, grief introduces us to its irresistible twin, joy. Grief and joy travel together and need each other. As the poet Mary Oliver writes: "We shake with grief, we shake with joy. What a time these two have, housed as they are in the same body."[2]

Regardless of how much we suffer, the joy that lives at our core cannot be extinguished.

๑๕๖

What has been your experience of finding joy in the midst of suffering?

GRIEF PRACTICES

A GRIEF TIMELINE

A practice that may be helpful is to create a grief timeline. This can be done using a pen and regular sheets of paper, but it is often useful to take a long sheet of butcher paper and attach it to a wall horizontally. Beginning at birth, trace the losses you can remember in your life by drawing a long horizontal line from the left side of the paper to the right. Take time to write each loss on the timeline and note your age at the time of the loss. The usefulness of the timeline is not in noting all the losses in one day, but rather coming back to the timeline regularly and adding the losses you remember. Think of the timeline not as a project that must be finished, but as an ongoing diary of your losses. This grief timeline can provide perspective and help you visually track the losses in your life. Often, having a visual record of losses is more substantial than merely thinking about them.

Additionally, you can journal about key points of grief recorded on the timeline.

TRACKING GRIEF IN THE BODY

Every human being on this planet is storing grief in their body. If we know where it is in the body and familiarize ourselves with the sensations of its energy in the body, we can gradually develop an intimate relationship with our grief that doesn't require us to do anything with it except be aware of it.

This practice is best done while lying down on the floor at a time and place where you are not likely to be interrupted. Take a few moments to get comfortable and practice taking 4-5 long, slow, deep breaths. Then beginning with the feet, slowly focus your attention on that part of the body. What sensations do you notice there? Whatever the sensations are, breathe into them gently. Then continue scanning upward slowly, focusing on the legs, buttocks, and abdomen. Notice the physical sensations and any pictures or images that might arise.

Continue slowly scanning the body upward focusing on the stomach, lower back, middle back, and upper back. Notice also the stomach and chest cavity. What are the sensations? Do any images arise?

Slowly continue scanning upward into the shoulders, throat, neck, jaw, and face. Notice the sensations and images. Then scan gently to the eyes and head.

When you have finished the scan, arise gently and write down the sensations and images you noticed in the scan.

PART THREE: JOY

Francis Weller writes that "we live in what I call a 'flat-line culture,' where the band is narrow in terms of what we let ourselves fully feel. We may cry at a wedding or when we watch a movie, but the full-throated expression of emotion is off-limits."[1] A flat-line culture is a numbed and numbing culture where we are not allowed to feel too happy because someone might call us or diagnose us as being "manic." Of course, if we openly express our grief, we might be called or diagnosed as "depressed." The culture prescribes a certain range of emotional expression to which we conform in order to appear "normal," and we generally behave within those parameters.

Another obvious interpretation of "flat-line culture" is that such a culture is dead. Its life-force has departed. Its inhabitants lack vitality, passion, and ardor. In other words, it has expired. Time of death...?

It requires centuries, decades, and years to produce a flatline culture. While we may attribute many causes to the condition, unquestionably, our inability to grieve contributes to the habitual numbing. Grief is a testimony to our vitality, and when we cannot grieve, we progressively become numb and semi-alive. When we are able to feel our grief, our capacity to feel all other emotions is enhanced. Most notably, when we cannot feel grief, we also cannot feel joy.

William Blake declared this centuries ago: "The deeper the sorrow, the greater the joy."[2] Conscious grieving enhances our capacity to feel joy, as well as a host of other emotions. However, we must understand the difference between joy and happiness and in doing so, discover our deepest humanity.

THE HAPPENSTANCE OF HAPPINESS

Joy is inexpressibly more than happiness.
Happiness befalls people; happiness is fate,
while people cause joy to bloom inside
themselves. Joy is plainly a good season for
the heart; joy is the ultimate achievement of
which human beings are capable. [1]
—Rainer Maria Rilke

If we examine the etymology of the word *happiness*, we notice that it is related to other words like *happen, haphazard,* and *happenstance.* That is because the root prefix, *hap,* pertains to fortune or chance. Sometimes we are fortunate enough to be happy, and at other times, we are, unfortunately, *un*-happy. Happiness comes and goes depending on our circumstances. Joy, however, is not circumstantial.

Many individuals have experienced moments of joy in the midst of misery and horror. Holocaust survivor Viktor Frankl is one example. Frankl was infused with joy in the moments when he found meaning and purpose in his suffering and when he noticed other inmates transitioning to a similar change in awareness. Nelson Mandela, Harriett Tubman, Helen Keller, Vaclav

Havel, Martin Luther King, Jr., and His Holiness, the Dalai Lama have reported similar encounters with joy while also feeling forsaken, persecuted, exiled, tortured, and frighteningly alone in their suffering.

Joy develops, not in the human ego, which often moves heaven and Earth to feel "happy." Rather, it becomes a reservoir of strength, courage, wisdom, empathy, and perseverance within us to which we can turn in moments of suffering and catastrophe. Joy may erupt in the context of happiness and celebration as well. Joy and happiness are not enemies, but we are not served by confusing the two or being deluded that happiness and joy are synonymous.

Joy is a deep, interior, inherent cellular-level experience of meaning, purpose, groundedness, and well-being. We can tap into it even in moments of grief, sorrow, anxiety, anger, fear, and despair.

❦

Have there been moments in your life when you felt joy, even when you were unhappy?

What were those moments like?

❧ 26 ❧

BARRIERS ON THE ROAD
TO JOY

The idea that we somehow have an obligation to be happy, should expect
happiness, or even have a right to be happy creates an invidious
phantasm that people chase numbly through all their years, feeling
cheated in the end not to have found it. The soul neither wants nor asks
for you to be happy: the soul wants you to live—fully, bodily, open to
passion and heartbreak and love and awakened to living vibrations of
the One. The pursuit of happiness is a soulless enterprise.
—Charles Upton, *Day and Night on the Sufi Path*[1]

Upton's words give us insight into the relationship
between joy and aliveness. In a dead (flatline) culture,
people are never fully alive. Hence their desperation
for happiness. Feeling happy often infuses us with moments of
circumstantial aliveness which later dwindle back into a
comatose, mechanical existence in search of the next infusion of
happiness.

As we have seen, not feeling one's feelings or monitoring how
much we feel, such as controlling grief and other emotions,
serves to anesthetize our bodies and calcify our hearts. The great
mythologist, Joseph Campbell, asserted, "People say that we're
searching for the meaning of life. I don't think that's it at all. I

think that what we're seeking is an experience of being alive, so that our life experiences on the purely physical plane will have resonances within our own innermost being and reality, so that we actually feel the rapture of being alive."[2]

Yet meaning and aliveness travel together and cannot be separated. "Dead" people often miss the meaning, whereas people who reverence meaning are usually extraordinarily alive.

Active, mystical hope, as well as cherishing our capacity to grieve, are the beating heart of the vitality of our species. When we are infused with these, a flat-line existence becomes intolerable, and a reservoir of joy replenishes the arid chasm of well-behaved, socially acceptable blandness within.

※

How has your resistance to grieving curtailed your aliveness?

Francis Weller entitled his book, The Wild Edge of Sorrow. *What is your "wild edge of sorrow"?*

❧ 27 ❧

RADICAL JOY FOR HARD
TIMES

*We are willing to face the sorrow we feel when the places we care about
have been hurt and to respond not by turning our backs but by boldly
stepping forth to spend time with these places and offer them gifts of love
and gratitude for all they have given to us. We believe that in these
troubling times, taking care of the places where we live in the present,
even as we work for a better future, is an essential tool for survival.*
—Trebbe Johnson, Founder of Radical Joy for Hard Times

On her website, Trebbe Johnson offers these words:

Have you ever been to a sacred site? What do you think of
when you consider that term? Paha Sapa, the land that is the
center of the universe for the Lakota people? Stonehenge?
Uluru in Australia?

Author Andrew Blackwell encountered a sacred site in what
seemed at first an unlikely place.

For his book, *Visit Sunny Chernobyl*, Blackwell visited some
of the most polluted places in the world, including the
Ukrainian site of the worst nuclear disaster in history, the tar
sands of Canada, and the great Pacific garbage patch. In India

he makes his way to the Najafgarh, a rivulet that flows through New Delhi, where it is confined to a channel that eventually empties into the Yamuna River. It is the Indian capital's most polluted water body, for it receives a constant influx of untreated sewage from the populous surrounding areas. Blackwell stares at all the wilted, snagged, washed up offerings that people have made there. So much attention and so much reference for a scummy canal filled with sewage!

"And why not?" Blackwell asks himself and us. "Underneath the stink and the noise, the rationale unfolded. This was a tributary of the Yamuna. Are you not to venerate it merely because it smells? Why not worship it, suspended solids and all? What could be more sacred than a river that springs from inside your neighbor's belly?"

What are the sacred places we ourselves might be ignoring simply because we have not paused long enough to look below the surface?[1]

❁

*Johnson's mission is to offer blessing
and radical joy to wounded places.*

*What is a place near you that you might visit and
bring your grief, your love, and your blessing?*

RADICAL JOY PRACTICES

Below are practices given on the Radical Joy for Hard Times website.[1] There is no copyright on these practices. They are intended to be read and used by anyone. Founder Trebbe Johnson wants all who are concerned about the state of our planet to engage with Radical Joy Practices and add their own as well in order to bring healing and wholeness to the Earth. In this way, we bear witness to the suffering and affirm for ourselves and the world that it mattered.

DIALOG WITH NATURE

Go outside—it doesn't matter where. Outside could be a wilderness area, your own backyard, or a vacant lot. Wander around with an attitude of meditative expectation, looking and listening for what attracts your attention and interest. After you've wandered for a while, stop and sit with one nature "being." This being could be a patch of crabgrass, a dead tree, a wildflower. Simply sit, noticing the details of this unique being that has called to you. Note its unique way of being itself. Note also the feelings and thoughts that arise within you as you consider it. Are you sad? Wistful? Happy? Does being there with that nature being remind you of any experience from your past? Talk to this being. Tell it what you see in it, how you feel about it. Then listen to what it has to say to you. Trust whatever comes to you. You will probably reach a point when you feel you've done enough, and you'll want to get up and leave. Resist the temptation! Stay there a little longer and continue to pay attention. When you leave, thank the being for calling to you and revealing something about itself—and about you.

NIGHT AND LIGHT

This exercise opens you up to the immensity and beauty of the night sky—as well as the human-made junk cluttering it up. Go outside at night and make yourself comfortable. Gaze into the sky. Note what stars and planets you see, and what phase the moon is in. Reflect on how this perspective of the universe makes you feel. Then turn your attention to the lights that come from human civilization, including city lights, planes, and satellites. How do you feel about them? Let your thoughts wander, refusing to be satisfied with first impressions or judgments alone.

SIMPLY BOW

Many times life simply does not permit us to spend time with wounded places or beings long enough to give them some attention. However, you can always take a small, simple action in honor of something that has been hurt or destroyed. This practice is especially useful if you're in a car and see an animal that has been killed by vehicular traffic. When you pass by, simply bow your head or when you are not driving in silent tribute. Thank the animal for its life.

MAKE A GIFT FOR A HURT PLACE

Visit an area where you know there has been damage to nature—human-made or natural. Sit quietly in this area, taking in the whole place. What is your first reaction? As you sit there for a while, note how your attention and your reactions shift. There is no right or wrong direction. Boredom is natural too! Do you notice only brokenness and ugliness or do you spot signs of beauty too? Or signs of nature rebounding after something has happened to it? What are these signs? How do they interact with the broken areas? Before you leave, make a gift for the place out of materials the place offers.

MAKE A GIFT FOR A HURT PLACE—THE NANO VERSION

When you are walking, you have a greater opportunity to pay a slightly longer tribute to a place or being that has been hurt than if you're driving. If you come upon an animal or a place that has been hurt, you can also Simply Bow before moving on. And, if time and circumstances permit, consider making a small gift of beauty. For example, you can lay a wildflower on the body of the animal, or make a small design out of sticks, leaves, and stones for a place.

CAIRN FOR LOST PLACES

When we learn about damage or threat to the natural world or to a place we love, we often feel overwhelmed by feelings of helplessness and despair. It seems there is nothing we can do with these feelings. This practice offers a small but tangible way of marking those difficult feelings and offering them up to the Earth of which we are all a part.

For the practice you will make a small cairn, a pile of stones. You can do it outside using field stones or in your house using pebbles or gravel. The point is to commemorate the threatened life of one of the Earth's citizens and your own feelings of sadness about it. Every time you hear or read that some place or species is under assault, place a stone on top of or around your cairn. Speak aloud the name of the place or species you are thinking of, whose existence is threatened. After you have placed your stone, pause long enough to reflect on the life of that being or place. In future, you might want to meditate before your cairn.

THANKING THE OUTSIDE INSIDE

No matter where you live, the natural world is part of your home. If you have house plants or pets, they may be the most obvious examples that come to mind. But there is probably wood in your house as well, in the windowsills or on tables and the legs of chairs. The pipes that supply water and heat are made of lead or copper. Sheep may have contributed to wool blankets. And of course, nature awaits your dining pleasure in your refrigerator. Open your awareness to the ways and forms that so many plants and animals have entered your home and your life. In these contemporary times, most of them are likely anonymous. Imagine the beings whose lives contributed to your well-being and thank them.

❧ 28 ❧

HOLDING THE TENSION OF
LIFE'S OPPOSITES

Everything is so beautiful, and I am so sad...
I am so sad, and everything is so beautiful.[1]
—Mark Nepo, *Adrift*

Western culture is tragically unfamiliar with paradox. Perhaps if it were, we would not be facing the predicament that now ensnares us. When a culture has *an I-Thou*, intimate relationship with nature, it more easily grasps the interconnectedness of everyone and everything. Companionship with the natural world dispels the illusion that living beings are separate from one another and that their ideas can be perceived dualistically.

In nature-based cultures, suffering is viscerally experienced as part of existence, facilitating the capacity to hold two opposite ideas in one's consciousness. Intimacy with nature instills in us the reality that beauty and sorrow are two different, but not divergent, experiences.

For this reason, both the unfolding collapse of industrial civilization and the paradigm on which it rests mystify industrially civilized humans. How could it be otherwise? Therefore, the writings and teachings of myself and others about holding the tension of opposites appear absurd to those whose worldview is fundamentally dualistic. One grandmother weeps for her infant grandchild who was just born onto a planet reeling from catastrophic climate change and fears for the child's future to such an extent that she has difficulty celebrating the birth—yet another part of her is ecstatic that her granddaughter has arrived. As she sits with the tension, she feels as if her body and soul are torn to pieces. The poet Mark Nepo wrote some of his best poetry while he was undergoing chemotherapy for cancer and was able to write the words above: *Everything is so beautiful, and I am so sad...I am so sad, and everything is so beautiful.*

Often, the only way citizens of Western culture can hold the tension of opposites is through experiencing one or more of the gates of grief. Typically, the dissolution of the barriers between "good" and "bad" happens in times of suffering if we are open to the possibility that in the deepest layers of our humanity, such labels are hollow and inconsequential.

☙❧

*Is there some tension of opposites that has been
or is gutting your heart and soul?*

A PRACTICE FOR HOLDING
THE TENSION OF OPPOSITES

When we are confronted with a situation in which two opposing ideas, feelings, or perspectives appear to be unresolvable because we believe we must choose which one is correct, one of the least useful responses is logical reasoning. Both opposites are true, so it is futile to approach them logically. What is needed is not a "right" or "wrong" response, but rather, the capacity to take both perspectives into our awareness and hold them closely. Something greater than the mind is required to take the opposites out of the oppositional field.

What may be useful is to consciously sit with the opposites utilizing the body and emotions.

Choose a quiet time and space where you will not be interrupted. Close your eyes. Now take at least 5 long, slow, deep breaths. Then see the opposing fields in front of you. Pay attention to each one separately, and notice the sensations in the body that arise as a result. Spend at least 2-3 minutes with the first one, noticing the possible outcome of this perspective. Then spend 2-3 minutes with the other, again noticing the possible outcome. Take plenty of time to witness the feelings and images that arise. Then take a mental step back from the opposites. Again, take another 5 long, slow deep breaths.

Now see both perspectives in front of you as if you were watching them on a movie screen. Take a few moments to focus on one of the perspectives, then quickly switch to focusing your attention on the other. Now quickly switch your attention back to the opposite perspective, then switch to the other. Do this at least 5 times or more—back and forth, from one opposite to the other. Notice the sensations in your body as you alternate your attention from one opposite to the other.

Now come back from your experience of alternating and take several long, slow, deep breaths. What do you notice? Have your body sensations changed? Both perspectives are still opposites, but as you have been sitting with them, has anything changed?

Take time to write in your journal about this exercise. If you find it useful, you may want to repeat it on another day.

❧ 29 ❧
BETWEEN HEARTBREAK AND ECSTASY

Our life is a short time in expectation, a time in which sadness and joy kiss each other at every moment. There is a quality of sadness that pervades all the moments of our life. It seems that there is no such thing as clear-cut pure joy, but that even in the happiest moments of our existence we sense a tinge of sadness. In every satisfaction, there is an awareness of its limitations. In every success, there is the fear of jealousy. Behind every smile, there is a tear. In every embrace, there is loneliness. In every friendship, distance. And in all forms of light, there is the knowledge of surrounding darkness.
—Henri Nouwen, *Out of Solitude*[1]

The Dutch Catholic priest and psychologist, Henri Nouwen, was conflicted throughout his entire adult life about his sexual orientation. Those of us who have spent even a portion of our lives struggling with this conflict can fully empathize with those who are torn apart by it. While I was able to resolve the inner altercation early in life, many never do, or like Nouwen, resolve it only in their last few years of life.

Perhaps struggling with a conflict so deep that it feels as if it is eviscerating the soul allows some individuals to experience on a cellular level a still point between heartbreak and ecstasy that facilitates holding the tension of opposites. On the other hand, one may be consumed by the turmoil for most of one's life, as Nouwen was. Yet in the words above, he demonstrates a deep awareness of the tension of opposites and the reality that each opposite lives within the other.

Those awakening to the depth and breadth of the polycrisis are profoundly impaired by our culturally programmed dualistic perspective. Therefore, the more we practice holding the tension of opposites and experiencing the ecstasy within the heartbreak and the sorrow within the joy, the less likely we are to be devastated by worldwide unraveling.

We can practice noticing the tinge of sadness within moments of joy, alongside the sweetness that pervades or quietly attends moments of grief and loss. Noticing such both-ands supports our capacity to hold and honor the opposites inherent in the dissolution of nature and culture.

Holding the opposites in our awareness not only expands our thinking, but it literally expands *us*. Our hearts and our psyches broaden and deepen. We become more of who we genuinely are. And perhaps that is the hidden gift in the demise.

❧ 30 ❧

MAKING MEANING IN A TIME
OF LOSS

Ends and beginnings may be polar opposites,
but like most opposed things, they are secretly connected.
Part of the revelation of the end-times is that things do not actually end
altogether. In the great drama of the world, the end leads back to the
beginning and, from what went before, things begin again.
—Michael Meade, *Why the World Doesn't End:*
Finding Renewal in a Time of Loss[1]

Michael Meade is a storyteller, author, and scholar of
mythology, anthropology, and psychology. The
following is my commentary on *Why the World
Doesn't End.*

Deeply influenced by the works of Carl Jung, Mircea Eliade,
Edith Hamilton, James Hillman, Malidoma Somé, and Joseph
Campbell, he views our world through a lens of myth, symbol-
ism, and the inextricable connection between nature and
culture. Meade's passion for making meaning and making sense
of humanity's predicament in a dark time reverberates
throughout *Why the World Doesn't End* as well as Meade's other
books, such as *The World Behind the World* (2008) and *Fate and
Destiny* (2010).

As an avid reader of Meade, it is nearly impossible for me to characterize his writing and storytelling in just one word, but if forced to do so, I would have to say "paradox." His work is replete with paradox and the capacity to hold the tension of opposites in order to facilitate a third option and thereby birth authentic transformation. For example, "finding renewal in a time of loss," or "a light inside dark times," or "the ends of time, the roots of eternity," are the names of a few of his book and CD titles.

In a time of decline, demise, unraveling and what is very likely to be the collapse of industrial civilization and the paradigm on which it rests, it is crucial to grasp and nourish the opposite of descent by attending to all that may facilitate an ascent to a rebirth of humanity. Descent, in fact, is only one half of the story of civilization that is now playing out its last act. From the ashes of that collapsed paradigm, another will emerge, and our work in current time is to forge a framework with which it can be constructed—a skeleton of sanity, sagacity, creativity, compassion, and vision to be enfleshed on the bare bones of what we modestly call "preparation," knowing that today's preparation is tomorrow's next culture.

The decline of civilization is occurring in the context of an obsession with all things new, innovative, and ostensibly original. Yet increasingly we are discovering that ancient, indigenous wisdom sustained other, more mature civilizations for longer periods of time, and many individuals and communities are avidly reclaiming and employing the myths of our ancestors in order to make sense of our predicament. Michael Meade is such an individual, whose work encompasses not only the realm of storytelling and writing but in-depth mentoring programs for at-risk youth and powerful healing retreats for returning combat veterans and their families.

So while I know that the *world* will not end, I also know that many things are ending. In fact, it appears that every institution constructed by our myriad societies is in a state of demise. Both nature and culture are hugely at risk as humanity has now created a climate emergency in which melting ice caps, rising sea levels, species extinction, famine, and drought appear to shape the catastrophic context of our imminent future. Whether human beings admit the reality of these endings, their ramifications register and reverberate in the nether regions of our psyches. For in fact, "apocalypse" is an archetype (universal theme) in the collective unconscious of the psyche. The problem with archetypes, however, is that while they consume enormous amounts of psychic energy, we never know exactly how they will play out. For this reason, myths and stories which have throughout time arisen from archetypes also contain clues about how best to navigate them.

As we well know, in a time of endings, we are all psychologically more vulnerable. Whether it is the death of a loved one, the ending of a relationship, the approach of retirement, a financial bankruptcy, or foreclosure on the place we call home, endings tend to generate emotional rawness. Thus, apocalyptic forecasts often reveal much more about us than the forecast itself. In such times we are open to "psychic invasions," says Meade, which I find curious in an era of "home invasions," as if the places within us and around us that have felt most secure in the past no longer provide safety. The poet William Butler Yeats speaks of a center that cannot hold as things fall apart.

A culture in decline reveals many things, and of course we must not forget that the literal meaning of *apocalypse* is "the unveiling." Generally, in collapse, a culture's shadow or underside is revealed, and in a society which prides itself in being rational and logical, it is not surprising to see ghastly eruptions of the irrational and a chilling madness that results in mass murder and an escalation of terrified people arming themselves in attempt to prevent further carnage. In more than half the states in the United States, it is no longer necessary to have a permit to carry a firearm, and the number of deaths from firearms in the US exceeds that of any other country.

Apocalypse is not only an unveiling, but a time of being in a state of "in-between-ness" that is neither a complete ending nor an authentic beginning. At the same time that collapse and destruction are occurring, so also are discovery and renewal and a re-inventing of what once was. "Ends and beginnings are secretly connected," says Meade, "but it takes a mythical mind and a metaphorical sense to see how one might lead to the other. Whenever the end seems near, the beginning is also close at hand." One of the roles of myth is to give life meaning. As Meade states, we are narrative beings who find our way by *storying* the world around us. The lack of mythical mind in the age of decline presents a challenge for humanity that causes many to go mad for lack of the capacity to make sense of monumental loss.

Myths are not facts that can be proven true, but throughout time they have proven valuable when people lose a sense of what is true and realize that reason alone cannot provide meaning. In fact, Meade often describes myth as "a series of lies that tells the truth." In other words, they are not accounts of historical events that took place in real time, but they are products of the imagination that resonate with our universal human experience of being inherent "meaning makers" as we navigate the vicissitudes of life. Modern culture, however, has been stunted in its capacity to do so because, as Meade notes, "modern cultures try to produce obedient citizens and life-long consumers instead of people who know the meaning and purpose of their own lives."

To be modern is to live in a soul-less world. *Soul* in this context is not a religious word, but rather, as Meade says, "our unique, inward style and way of being in this world." Nevertheless, the enormous gift in this time of loss and seeming meaninglessness is that soul can be grown amid the chaos and collapse because "the threat of collapse and utter loss can also provide a deeper sense of wholeness when nothing but total involvement and wholeheartedness will work... In this darker revelation, things become both impossible and more possible at the same time."

In recent years I have committed my life to assisting my fellow earthlings in preparing emotionally and spiritually for a daunting and chaotic future which is clearly manifesting its implications in the present. While I am a student of myth and imagination, my perspective is often more literal than Meade's, yet I am aware that for the most part, spiritual preparation is about making sense of one's experience, both as an individual and as part of a community. My work takes me to people and places where the hunger for meaning and the capacity to make meaning with one's community is not only palpable but often astonishes me as I witness the lengths some human beings are willing to travel within themselves and with one another in order to reclaim the ancient wisdom that enables them to re-imagine their world.

In this time of "betwixt and between," this time of shifting from an either/or to a both/and perspective, it is crucial to logically analyze our predicament and then logistically prepare for it as much as humanly possible. To do so by definition brings one into philosophical and psychological conflict with the culture. A feeling of dissociation or schizophrenia is an invariable result. Likewise, when one witnesses a culture whose inhabitants are marinated in both apathetic denial and substantial levels of trauma at the same time, it is virtually impossible not to feel overwhelmed. As Michael Meade writes, "Periods of radical change either develop maturity in people or else cause them to regress."

In the second section of *Why the World Doesn't End*, Meade tells and comments on a number of ancient stories that offer grounded wisdom and meaning for those wanting to make sense of the chaos of current time. Many of these are delightful stories of endings or challenges that pit individuals between poles of opposites that test their resolve and bring forth a third, transformative force which resolves the situation in an unexpected, so-called "irrational" manner. I highly recommend a journey into the paradox, playful humor, and profound parables that *Why the*

World Doesn't End offers the reader. In this dark time, one is illumined by a quality of irreverent inspiration and renewal only found in a mythopoetic perspective. For as Michael Meade asserts:

> When the world becomes darker the inner light of the soul becomes more important; when even nature seems about to unravel the inner pattern, the thread of meaning can be the only way to feel woven into life and bound for some valuable purpose that can assist the world in distress. When the world becomes dark with endings it becomes time to turn to the inner thread that first brought each soul to this life. Although it cannot be found by common observers, as long as we hold the inner thread of being, we cannot be completely lost in this world.

❧

What is your "thread of meaning"?
How are you making sense of our predicament?

❧ 31 ❧

THE JOY OF MAKING
MEANING

Meaning making is wounding.
—Robert Orsi, *Between Heaven and Earth:*
The Religious Worlds People Make
and the Scholars Who Study Them[1]

I t is tempting when speaking of finding or making meaning,
to assume that if we can make meaning as we contemplate
the demise of industrial civilization, we will be at peace.
Our dilemmas will be resolved, and all will be well internally and
externally. However, meaning is neither found nor made without
a price. All of those "assignments" that Stephen Jenkinson challenges us to take on which we considered in the Hope section of
this book are not embraced without a cost. In order to accept
the assignment, we must be willing to be vulnerable, and when
we are vulnerable, we risk feeling pain.

We cannot make meaning if we do not look with unsparing
honesty at the shadow—the one within us and the one perme-
ating every corner of our culture. Shadow work is painful. As we
refuse to close our eyes to the devastation of nature wrought by
other humans and enabled by us, we sometimes feel engulfed in
fear, anger, and grief.

Since climate chaos, and the inevitable collapse of ecosystems because the human population has exceeded the carrying capacity of Earth, are both existential matters, threatening our own lives and the lives of our descendants, we are compelled to stare into the abyss of death and potential human extinction.

Yet it is precisely our willingness to be wounded by making meaning that also allows joy to erupt in some corner of the psyche or some unlikely patch of ground in our community. Since there is no "one" universal meaning to be made in the midst of suffering, death and loss almost always catapult us into the territory of soul and compel us to viscerally experience the deepest regions of what it means to be human. It is there that we are immersed in the "betwixt and between." Grief and joy, those two so-called "opposites," shimmer together as one.

❧

What does making meaning in apocalyptic times do for you?
How does it support you in the midst of uncertainty,
fear, grief, and despair?

PART FOUR: CARING

Service brings us joy. Over the years, I've interviewed people who participated in disaster relief. I've always been astonished to notice that no matter how tragic and terrible the disaster, they always spoke of that experience with joy. They've led me to realize that there is nothing equal to helping other people. In service, we discover profound happiness. We all witnessed this in the days after September 11, 2001. A comment that still brings tears to my eyes was made by a survivor who said: "We didn't save ourselves. We tried to save each other."

The joy and meaning of service is found in every spiritual tradition. It was once expressed very simply to me: "All happiness in the world comes from serving others; all sorrow in the world comes from acting selfishly."
—Margaret Wheatley[1]

❧ 32 ❧

CARING SKILLFULLY IN A
COLLAPSING WORLD

My religion is kindness.
—His Holiness, the Dalai Lama

Regardless of our circumstances, if we have food, shelter, and safety, it is our nature to care for other living beings. Even houseless people care for their pets. In fact, our humanity is deepened by caring, even if it is only for a goldfish.

But in a collapsing world—a world wrought with trauma, unpredictability, danger, hunger, thirst, and illness (both physical and mental), caring for ourselves and for others may become formidable. Natural disasters compel us to care about the wellbeing of our neighbors and mutually assist each other in a time of crisis. In extreme crises, particularly if a community or neighborhood becomes a war zone of violence or disease, individual survival becomes the priority, not looking after one another.

For this reason, caring for one another within healthy boundaries should become a daily practice. As we prepare ourselves emotionally and spiritually for an increasingly broken world, we must teach ourselves and others how to care, how to be kind, and how to live within the limits of nature's grace. I believe that shadow work and practicing compassion are extraordinary curricula for creating a culture based on care and deep community.

Many of us who have not known boundaries around caring become enablers or codependent with the people we care for. Often in the process we discover that in the name of caring, we have been meeting our own needs for control, people-pleasing, or self-esteem building by ignoring our own limits or the limits of others.

As societies deteriorate, the need for caring may become overwhelming. We may need to demonstrate caring to people we do not particularly like or who do not like us. We may need to be cared for and become vulnerable with people we do not know well and with whom we have not developed trust.

However, if any possibility exists for more evolved societies to be born from the collapse of civilization, they must be based on caring for each other. War-torn and disease-ridden nations have experienced the heartbreak that engenders care and causes human beings to rise to occasions they previously thought unfathomable.

Why do we care? We care because we *are* each other. Whether it is Jesus of Nazareth declaring, "Truly I tell you, whatever you did for one of the least of these brothers and sisters of mine, you did for me," or the Dalai Lama who asserts, "My religion is kindness," we care for one another because there is no separation between us ontologically or spiritually. In a state of unraveling, a hyper-individualistic culture such as that of the United States will no doubt learn this lesson brutally and unambiguously.

☙❦❧

- *From your perspective, what would a society organized around care look like? Take plenty of time to reflect on this.*

- *In a collapsed or collapsing society, what kinds of care can you offer? What kinds of care can you offer now?*
- *How might you need to be cared for in a severely disrupted world?*
- *What have been your experiences of caring and being cared for during the pandemic?*

❦ 33 ❦

FOLLOW THE HEARTBREAK

In the aftermath of any apocalypse, whether individual or collective, our most natural response as a result of the suffering we have experienced is to be infused with empathy and to wonder how we might alleviate the suffering of other sentient beings. Assuming that we survive a wildfire that destroys our neighborhood and engulfs our own home, we quite naturally want to help others who have lost their homes, even as we try to salvage whatever we can from our own home. We feel devastated by the deaths of our neighbors who could not escape in time. Our hearts break not only for the loss of our own home, but for our neighbors who have lost theirs. Our hearts are shattered not only by the loss of human life, but by the death and wounding of innocent animals.

Surviving a cataclysmic natural disaster is soul-crushing under the best of circumstances and always profoundly life-altering. But our hearts can be broken and our empathy ignited in situations much less catastrophic.

When our perspective of hope is modified, when our acceptance of descent becomes palpable, when our discernment of the difference between joy and happiness is clarified, and we discover that joy is the very core of our being—our passion for service often becomes unstoppable. But authentic service is not conjured from logic or mental prescriptions about what we "should" do. It effortlessly erupts from the body, particularly from a broken heart.

Rumi believed that heartbreak is necessary for heart-opening, and he also believed that the human heart can contain much more heartbreak than our minds imagine it can. We often say that some people die of a broken heart, and that is true—but almost always because they are unable to cherish the power of heartbreak as a result of neglect, abuse, or violence.

Whatever is breaking our hearts in this seemingly endless era of loss, follow the heartbreak and let it reveal where you are most needed.

۞

Now that you are becoming who you want to be in this demise, ponder more deeply: What did you come here to do?

✿ 34 ✿
LARGE-SCALE CHANGE, SMALL-SCALE RELATIONSHIPS

In spite of current ads and slogans, the world doesn't change one person at a time. It changes as networks of relationships form among people who share a common cause and vision of what's possible. This is good news for those of us who want to change public education. We don't need to convince large numbers of people to change; instead, we need to connect with kindred spirits.
—Meg Wheatley, "Working With Emergence"[1]

I n this culture, when most people consider change around any crisis, they assume that change must be made on a large scale. For decades, environmentalists have been trying to awaken the world to climate chaos by engaging the United Nations through international climate change conferences. Extinction Rebellion in Europe has organized countless protests to awaken the masses to the threat of species extinction as a result of climate chaos.

Many scientists and informed students of global warming, including myself, now assert that large-scale change globally is highly unlikely because it is too late to stop the devastating effects of climate chaos. The sanest response, it seems, are smaller efforts to mitigate climate catastrophe locally.

However, not everyone is drawn to engage directly with climate chaos mitigation. Many are called to serve in the areas of social justice, healthcare, animal rescue, immigration, homelessness, and countless other endeavors. While some individuals are committed to birthing organizations or businesses that provide service, most of us are drawn to serve in other ways.

However we choose to engage in service, we must remember that significant and lasting changes happen through webs of human relationships. Meg Wheatley emphasizes that:

> This is why networks are so important. But networks aren't the whole story. They need to evolve into intentional working relationships where new knowledge, practices, courage, and commitment can develop, such as happens in Communities of Practice. From these relationships, emergence becomes possible. Emergence is the process by which all large-scale change happens on this planet. Separate, local efforts connect and strengthen their interactions and interdependencies. What emerges as these become stronger is a system of influence, a powerful cultural shift that then greatly influences behaviors and defines accepted practices...
>
> In all living systems (which includes us humans), change always happens through emergence. Large-scale changes that have great impact do not originate in plans or strategies from on high. Instead, they begin as small, local actions. While they remain separate and apart, they have no influence beyond their locale. However, if they become connected, exchanging information and learning, their separate efforts can suddenly emerge as very powerful changes, able to influence a large system. This sudden appearance, known as an emergent phenomenon, always brings new levels of capacity. Three things are guaranteed with emergent phenomena. Their power and influence will far exceed any sum of the separate efforts. They will exhibit skills and capacities that were not present in the local efforts. And their appearance always surprises us.[2]

Additionally, networking in this way is only the first step. Individuals must move beyond it and commit to working together because there are more benefits and more concrete rewards in doing so.

While this sounds sensible and even appealing, let's notice the opportunity it presents for each person's individual shadow to be triggered within the context of intra-groups committing to work together. All manner of disagreements and projections are guaranteed to arise. The work then becomes a two-fold challenge involving both external service in the world through group engagement and inner work with one's shadow and one's psychological wounding. In fact, if both forms of work are not ongoing, one's capacity to make a difference in the world will be impeded and group commitments potentially sabotaged.

❦

External service brings joy and meaning.
It also brings a mirror that demands our attention.

❧ 35 ❧

OCCUPY SPIRITUALITY

*A spirituality that is only private and self-absorbed, one devoid of an
authentic political and social consciousness, does little to halt the suicidal
juggernaut of history. On the other hand, an activism that is not purified
by profound spiritual and psychological self-awareness and rooted in
spiritual truth, wisdom, and compassion will only perpetuate the problem
it is trying to solve, however righteous its intentions.*
—Andrew Harvey, *The Hope: A Guide To Sacred Activism* [1]

A dam Bucko and Matthew Fox wrote *Occupy Spirituality:
A Radical Vision for a New Generation* in 2013. Inspired by
the Occupy Wall Street movement, this book is about
the intuition that young people have been feeling for some time
now "...the intuition that we have a whole new generation of
young people who are finding themselves in a world that doesn't
feel like home anymore... A world that feels more like a hospital:
a hospital of broken institutions, systems, and also broken
human souls. And, that this situation requires our response, a
response that is deep and all encompassing, a spiritual response
if you will...Also, young people are feeling that this spiritual
response will most likely not come from the religious institutions which seem to be more concerned with self-preservation,

making sure that people have right beliefs, and that are too involved in maintaining the status quo. So young people are realizing that they are on their own..."[2]

Bucko and Fox articulate their perspective of Sacred Activism and the myriad ways activism can be embedded in spirituality and vice-versa. While many churches and religious institutions are providing for the needs of the poor and all manner of humans and animals who are suffering globally, younger generations have lost faith in religious efforts to do so. At the same time, many young people are familiar with other traditions besides Christianity and would like to incorporate those into their activism. Still other youth do not identify with any tradition, but still want to actively practice compassion and service.

Matthew Fox writes,

> Spiritual democracy seeks out wisdom from every source while not demanding that one abandon his or her religious or cultural lineage. A certain religious humility can be learned—as I wrote in my book, *The Coming of the Cosmic Christ* 28 years ago. In the context of creation, all religions become more equal. There is no such thing as a Roman Catholic rainforest or a Buddhist ocean or an atheist river or a Baptist moon or a Lutheran sun. In the context of the Sacred, all traditions have something to teach us and still, along with science, we have to seek wisdom everywhere including from nature itself.[3]

Are you motivated to service or activism by any particular tradition?

❦ 36 ❧

THE BODHISATTVA WARRIOR

Look at the teachings about the bodhisattva. The bodhisattva is the heroic figure who was modeled on the Buddha, one who really gets how interconnected we all are, like cells in a larger body. Then, when something affects that larger body, and other people are suffering, the bodhisattva is the one who is described as having a boundless heart, a huge heart—a compassionate one who feels the suffering not only of herself or himself, but of other beings, too. So the bodhisattva experiences a shift in identity or an extension into a larger self.
—Joanna Macy[1]

The Bodhisattva in Buddhist tradition is anyone who embraces the world in their heart with compassion. They see the suffering of the world and consciously embrace it by being aware of what they are feeling about it and remaining brave enough to face it. In order to do this, we must remind ourselves that we are all going to die. We are limited and finite beings. Remembering that all living beings are going to die enables us to feel with all who are suffering. What flows naturally from seeing the suffering of ourselves and others is compassion, or as Joanna Macy says, "Compassion is what impels you to act for the sake of the larger whole—or put more accurately, it is the whole acting through you."[2]

In facing suffering, the ego instinctively reacts with judgment —judgment of the ones suffering and judgment of those who contributed to the suffering. However, the Bodhisattva notices their reactivity and returns to focusing on compassion. The persons suffering may have made bad choices, but they are suffering nevertheless. Unkind people may have caused their suffering, but the Bodhisattva must work to alleviate the suffering rather than fixate on the persons who caused it. That does not mean that the Bodhisattva is passive about the causes of suffering or ignores them. He or she still seeks justice.

Not only must we embody the archetype of the Bodhisattva, but also that of the Shambhala Warrior. The hallmark of that warrior is moral and physical courage. Compassion and insight are their two principal weapons.

Joanna explains that,

> Compassion by itself can burn us out. So we need the second as well, which is insight into the dependent co-arising of all things. It lets us see that the battle is not between good people and bad people, for the line between good and evil runs through every human heart. We realize that we are interconnected, as in a web, and that each act with pure motivation affects the entire web, bringing consequences we cannot measure or even see. But insight alone can seem too cool to keep us going. So we need as well the heat of compassion, our openness to the world's pain. Both weapons or tools are necessary to the Shambhala warrior.[3]

Neither the Bodhisattva nor the Shambhala Warrior obsesses about the results of their efforts. They act on their compassion and courage simply because it is the right thing to do, and because they are motivated by forces within themselves more compelling than "results."

To act in this way is the most authentic expression of hope.

❦

*In what ways have you expressed or are you expressing the Bodhisattva?
In what ways have you expressed or are you expressing the Shambhala
Warrior?
In what ways are you being called to express these in response to our
global predicament?
What are your concerns about doing so?*

BECOMING A GOOD ANCESTOR

We all have ancestors, known and unknown, from the immediate pool of ancestors or from the larger pool of ancestors. The immediate pool of ancestors is our direct family members, our grandparents, our great-grandparents. And the pool of ancestors would be the trees, the rocks, the birds, [and] all of those amazing leaders who we have loved, like Gandhi and Martin Luther King Jr. and Harriet Tubman. Those are part of the pool of ancestors—not our immediate ancestors, but part of the pool of ancestors that we can all work with. Those are the kind of spirits I'm asking them to bring forward.
—Sobonfu Somé, elder of the Dagara Tribe, Burkina Faso[1]

An integral aspect of indigenous cultures is reverence for one's ancestors. Overall, modern cultures do not share the same depth of reverence for ancestors. Once an ancestor has died, we generally believe, we have no connection with them, nor do our descendants have any relationship with us once we have died.

Conversely, in traditional cultures, one has an eternal relationship both with one's ancestors and with one's descendants. Moreover, as a young person in those cultures matures, they are repeatedly reminded to respect and call on the help of their ancestors and to live their lives in present time in a manner that will enrich and support their descendants.

But how does one live in apocalyptic times with the support of one's ancestors and also live as a benevolent ancestor for one's descendants?

First, we must know that we are profoundly influenced by our ancestors, even if we have never met them. As a result, we are both impacted by their trauma, and at the same time, we can call upon them for assistance in current time, even if they were less than decent human beings. Traditional cultures assert that transition from this life to the next is inherently purifying and brings forth the authentic Self of all who pass through it. What is more, our ancestors are not only the humans in our lineage: there are other beings of nature, such as animals, birds, trees, rivers, and rocks.

Secondly, even if we have never considered it, we can call on our ancestors in their myriad forms for assistance, and we can begin even now to become wise ancestors for our descendants. For most of us, this means "coming of age at the end of an age."

Thirdly, even if we do not have children, we are becoming ancestors with regard to the kind of society we are leaving to younger generations and the service in which we are presently engaged. Our behavior and our decisions must consider the consequences for at least the next seven generations.

Consider these qualities, not only of a wise ancestor, but also of a wise elder who serves the community in real time, as well as their descendants:

- Consider that you are a link in a magnificent chain. It is not your responsibility to solve the issues of the polycrisis in this lifetime. However, it is your responsibility to become a wise elder.
- You cannot become a wise elder without working to heal your trauma. What we do not heal, we pass on.

- Be willing to grieve the losses of our time and make friends with grieving as part of your human journey.
- Savor the joy that comes from deep grieving and share it in order to heal wounded people and wounded places.
- Cultivate deep wisdom and deep compassion.
- Honor the stories of your ancestors and tell them to your descendants and your community. Be an honorable part of the stories you want your descendants to tell their children.
- Be a custodian of the Earth. Deepen your connection with Earth so that you can model stewardship of it.

❦

What steps are you taking to become a good ancestor?
How are you cultivating deeper wisdom and becoming a wise elder?

$ 38 $

CREATING A
COUNTERCULTURE OF CARE

*Creating a counterculture of care means practicing patience and
extending compassion much more often than we are inclined to. It means
that our work exists in opposition to policing, bondage and bordering. It
also means grieving our losses, for our own sakes, in order to heal and
hold onto our humanity, and because unprocessed trauma is a destructive
force. People are already doing this work, and some have been doing it for
generations. In that work, in those relationships, in that creativity, I see a
lot of hope, and room for a lot of joy.*
—Shane Burley, *Why We Fight: Essays on Fascism, Resistance, and
Surviving the Apocalypse*[1]

In the fall of 2022, I created, with my colleague Eric Garza,
Founder of Quillwood Academy, an online study group
around the book I had published earlier that year,
*Undaunted: Living Fiercely into Climate Chaos in an Authoritarian
World.* At the request of participants, we created a follow-up
group for going deeper in our study, and in doing so, we gained
more participants.

As you know, above I have offered many of my own ideas
about hope, and those of others. My intention was to redefine
the word and transform the delusional definition of the word

that this culture has provided for us into skillful, vibrant action in the world, holding our calling close to our hearts, as well as each other. I had the joy of bearing witness to this kind of transformation in our *Undaunted* study groups. In any apocalyptic scenario, I would call on any member of the group for assistance in a heartbeat, and I would not hesitate to help them if they needed it from me.

However, the transformation I witnessed did not happen magically as people parked themselves in front of a Zoom screen for a couple dozen sessions. It happened as people interacted with the material in *Undaunted* and did so *with each other*. In other words, they did a deep dive into themselves and into caring community.

Every single participant was a caring person when they joined the group, but their depth of caring and compassion increased as a result of their group experience. That unfolded as a result of each person's commitment to engage with other group members, as well as their own inner practices.

In fact, there is no other way to create a community of caring.

I do not know what you will need as systems rapidly and frighteningly unravel. Nor do you know what I will need, but we can only be there for ourselves and for each other by doing the work that the polycrisis is shrieking and pleading for us to do.

APPENDIX

PSYCHO-SPIRITUAL PRACTICES FOR
NAVIGATING THE POLYCRISIS

For the past 15 years in my work related to the polycrisis, no words are more familiar to me than: *What should we do?*

Individuals in denial of our predicament may ask the question sarcastically with bemused scorn, asking only in anticipation of a response even more seemingly ridiculous than the assertion that industrial civilization is collapsing. Individuals who are awake to the polycrisis often ask the question in honest and fearful anticipation of the unraveling, or from a heartfelt desire to fortify themselves in order to navigate it.

Without exception, the question arises wherever I offer my work, and it is the primary impetus for writing this book. However, I am well aware that you can lead a horse to water, as the saying goes, but you can't make it drink. Anyone awake to our predicament is wise to hunger and thirst for practices, but tools are useless unless one deploys them. Sometimes people enjoy collecting practices for "the day when," but aren't actually willing to engage with them until they are engulfed in suffering.

I view this book as a kind of training manual for psycho-spiritual boot camp, but we must never forget that boot camp occurs *before* the conflagration, not after it.

Having said that, I offer these practices for those who are

awake to the polycrisis and are willing to engage with them as spiritual warriors, not as listless lookie-loos. Or in the words of Pema Chodron:

> A warrior accepts that we can never know what will happen to us next. We can try to control the uncontrollable by looking for security and predictability, always hoping for the comfortable and safe. But the truth is that we can never avoid uncertainty.[1]

Following are prompts for journaling, as well as contemplative exercises which can be utilized for sitting quietly with a particular question or statement in order to bring unconscious material to our awareness for the purpose of healing and developing emotional and spiritual resilience. Both kinds of exercises should be done in a quiet place without interruptions or distractions.

Begin contemplative practices by taking time to sit quietly with eyes closed and take four long, deep, slow breaths before engaging in any practice. When you have finished contemplating, take a few more deep breaths.

ADDITIONAL JOURNALING

- What are my greatest fears in relation to humanity's demise?
- What emotion am I feeling right now?
- Why might I be feeling this way?
- How was my fear responded to when I was a child?
- When I think of feeling powerless, what is the first memory that comes to mind?
- When I think of feeling strong and in command, what is the first memory that comes to mind?

- What do I need in this moment and what can I do to meet that need?
- Who are my allies as I commit to being Undaunted and Living Fiercely?
- When I let myself feel sad, do I sometimes feel better afterward?
- Do I know the difference between joy and happiness?
- What are my fears about grieving?
- What messages have I received from my family and culture about grief?
- What is it like for you to live in uncertainty around anything but especially our planetary predicament?
- What do you know about your shadow? How does it show up in your life? Draw a picture of it.
- How are you practicing compassion in your life? How are you practicing it with yourself?
- How do you feel about your own death? Take plenty of time to journal about this.

CONTEMPLATE AND PRACTICE

Following are questions to sit with and practices for grounding in an increasingly groundless world:

- What emotions am I feeling right now about the polycrisis?
- Take time to feel them briefly. What is it like for you to actually pay attention to the emotions?
- What is my sorrow about our planetary predicament?
- Take a few moments to sit with your sorrow. What do you notice?
- Notice what you feel around people who do not understand or refuse to understand the severity of our predicament. Experiment with spending some time with one of those individuals, and focus only on your

interaction with them as another human being. Do not talk about the polycrisis, and allow yourself to notice what you like about them and your relationship with them.

- In the Descent section of this book, you had the opportunity to learn more about your shadow. In the journaling section above this section, you had the opportunity to journal about it. I highly recommend journaling before doing the following practice. After having thought about your shadow through journaling, sit quietly with eyes closed and invite an image of your shadow to appear. It may be the same or a different image from other images you have had of it in the past. Slowly and gently ask the shadow to speak to you about what it wants from you. What does it say? Take time to listen. How do you feel about its message or messages to you? If you feel drawn to journal about your experience, do that.

- Join with a friend or a group of friends who understand our planetary predicament and visit a "wounded place" as you read about in the section above on Joy. Choose one or more of the practices in that section of the book to engage in with your friend or friends.

- A Gratitude/Giving Practice: We can practice gratitude by making mental or written lists of people, things, and situations for which we are grateful. We can also put our gratitude into action by actively giving as a way of saying "thank you."

*Every day, practice giving something to someone. It could be a compliment, a kindness, an object, a parking space, a tip, a place in line, some food, and more.

*Every month, we can make a contribution to a favorite charity or cause we hold dear. Giving and gratitude are inextricably connected because the more we give from a place of generosity, the more abundance comes to us in the natural flow of energy exchange.

NATURE IMMERSION PRACTICE

For one week, spend at least one hour wandering in nature per day. You may choose a different place each day or the same one. This means walking, not driving, and thus, dressing appropriately. Allow yourself to experience the sights, sounds, smells, textures, colors, light, and shadow of this place. Enter it innocently as if you have never been there before. Notice your tendency to label, intellectualize, and analyze your environment. Instead, set your intention to wander with your senses open and vulnerable. Prioritize communing with nature, rather than classifying it. Feel free to speak to trees, flowers, bodies of water, and animals. Allow them to speak to you.

A NATURE MEDITATION, FROM DAY SCHILDKRET

Set a timer, or just go for as long as you want.
Take your seat.
Just let your body meet the Earth.
Feel the weight and gravity pulling you closely to her.
Perhaps even imagine you have roots emerging from your tailbone,
and they begin to descend into the deep dark soil.
Let your skin take this place in.
Notice the temperature on your arms.
Notice if there is any breeze upon your face.
Is the sunlight bringing heat to your body?
Let your ears take this place in.

Do you hear the wind rustling the trees,
Or the buzzing of any insects,
Or perhaps the sound of a distant dog bark,
Or humans speaking?
Let your nose take in this place.
Feel the air enter your nostrils.
What does this place smell like?
Do the trees give off their spicy scent?
Does the ocean have a particular smell?
Or maybe you are in a place that also carries
the scent of human-made machines.
Where does this smell transport you?
Let your eyes take in this place and zoom wide.
Soften your gaze and take in the entire place.
The contours of her landscape,
the colors that appear in your gaze,
the shadows dancing all around you,
the place where the sky meets the Earth.
What is moving?
What stays still?
Do you see anyone watching you?
Let your eyes take in the place and get focused.
Narrow your gaze and focus on one thing.
Maybe it's the texture of the bark right in front of you,
Or one single blade of grass recently cut.
Let your eyes notice all the details.
The color of that particular thing.
Its shape and movement.
How unique and utterly itself it is.
Spend one more moment beholding this place.
Let it change before you.
Witness the light come and go.
Consider how long this place has looked the way it does.
Who else was here yesterday?
Or last year?

Or 100 years ago?
Or 10,000 years ago?
Or 10 million years ago?
Let yourself wonder what this place may be after you leave it.
Once again, feel yourself sitting in this spot,
your body meeting the Earth's body.
Relax.
Feel those roots of yours.
Still reaching far down into the body of that place.
Sense how grounded
and held
and present you are.

Give thanks for this place,
in the way you know how.
For the more you can sense her aliveness,
the more you can sense your own.

Let yourself slowly rise to your feet and walk from that place,
still aware that you're walking.
On her.

✻

"THE DIRECTIVE" BY MAYA SPECTOR

Here is the directive:
>   No matter what is coming
>   No matter what is here.
>   No matter what you feel.
>   No matter what you fear.
Sing!
Lift your head and sing
>   To the sky and the tall trees.

Bow your head and sing
> To the earth and the tender
> green shoots raising their heads
> after the rains.

No matter if you can't carry a tune
No matter if you wake up raspy-throated
> and hoarse

No matter what your feeble excuse,
> Sing your morning prayers.
> Sing your evening prayers.
> Sing just because.

Even if you only sing a silent song
> inside your own head

Even if all you do is hum, or chant
> your little walking song

The earth and this life.
> are so worthy of praise.

And what better way to praise
> than to sing?

Written and published by Mayor Spector in Distilled, by Maya Spector, 2023, Oakland, California/ www.barryandmayaspector.com

❧

"FALLING" BY LARRY ROBINSON

Falling
In these awe-filled days of fire and flood and plague
We watch and wait and wonder
When that fierce hand
Might reach at last for us.
Those of us not yet touched by calamity
Quake, knowing in our bones

That though we may be spared
This time, time will level us all.
No magic amulets, no prayers, no masks,
Good deeds or good looks
Can promise protection
From our terminal human condition.
And those who have watched a child
Swept forever from our arms
Or fled the flames that swallowed
Our hopes and our memories
Or hid from the bombs or the virus
Or the predator's gaze
Know that nothing now will ever be the same -
As if anything ever were.
For all of us are falling
Like ashes, like rain,
Like petals, like leaves;
But we all are falling together.
And if we knew, in truth,
There was nowhere to land,
Tell me: could we know the difference
Between falling and flying?

ADDITIONAL RESOURCES

- *Radical Regeneration: Sacred Activism and the Renewal of the World*, Andrew Harvey and Carolyn Baker, published by Inner Traditions, November, 2022. This book is a quartet comprised of four books that Andrew Harvey and I wrote together from 2016-2021. They are: *Return to Joy; Savage Grace; Saving Animals from Ourselves; Radical Regeneration.*
- *The Wild Edge of Sorrow*, by Francis Weller, and all writings and videos by Francis on grief.
- "Warriors of the Human Spirit" Leadership Training with Meg Wheatley[1]
- Sounds True "Healing Trauma" Online Course[2]
- The work of Dr. Gabor Maté[3]
- Understanding Polyvagal Theory, Dr. Stephen Porges Training and Resources[4]

GRATITUDES

- I am profoundly grateful that I have the opportunity to offer this book as a culmination of my efforts in the past 15 years to not only awaken readers to our global predicament, but provide tools for preparing oneself emotionally and spiritually for the inevitable.

- I am deeply appreciative of John Mabry and Apocryphile Press for "getting it" and publishing two of my titles prior to this one. Additionally, I am indebted to the wise ones who have inspired me— Joanna Macy, Francis Weller, Malidoma and Sobonfu Somé, Martin Prechtel, Mark Nepo, Michael Dowd, Margaret Wheatley, Richard Rohr, Matthew Fox, Pema Chodron, Stephen Jenkinson, and Trebbe Johnson.

- I am endlessly indebted to my dear friend and writing partner, Andrew Harvey and to Carl Jung, Meg Pierce, Randy Morris, and Jennifer Gordon.

- I bow also to my more-than-human writing companions, Ethel, Sammy, and Gordon. Your spirits quietly reverberate in our writing cave every day.

- I am deeply humbled by my readers and subscribers to the Daily News Digest who have savored and promoted my work from the beginning.

- I thank my mother for teaching me to read and write and my father for loving me in spite of the countless Inquisitions he believed I deserved.

- I bow in love and service to this gorgeous, glorious, magnanimous planet that we no longer deserve, but who loves and cares for us as best she can anyway.

NOTES

EPIGRAPH

1. Mark Nepo, *Surviving Storms,* St. Martins Press, 2022.

1. WHAT IS HOPE?

1. Joanna Macy, Chris Johnstone: *Active Hope (revised): How to Face the Mess We're in with Unexpected Resilience and Creative Power,* New World Library, 2022.

2. MYSTICAL HOPE

1. Stephen Jenkinson, "Strangers of Kindness," https://orphanwisdom.com/2016/10/06/strangers-of-kindness/

3. HOPE IS NOT OPTIMISM

1. David McWilliams, "No Hope For Blind Optimism," Oct 4, 2010, http://davidmcwilliams.ie/no-hope-for-blind-optimism/
2. Vaclav Havel, *Disturbing The Peace: A Conversation with Karel Huizdala,* 1991.

4. ABANDON HOPE

1. [1] Pema Chodron: *When Things Fall Apart,* Shambala, 2016

5. A DISHEARTENING DUO: HOPE AND FEAR

1. Margaret Wheatley, "The Place Beyond Hope and Fear," PDF, 2009, https://www.margaretwheatley.com/articles/BeyondHopeandFear.pdf

6. HOPE AND THE OPPRESSION OF OUTCOME

1. Letter to a Young Activist, February 21, 1966.
2. Margaret Wheatley, "The Place Beyond Hope and Fear," PDF, 2009, https://www.margaretwheatley.com/articles/BeyondHopeandFear.pdf

7. HOPE IS THE ENEMY OF GRIEF

1. Dahr Jamail, "In Facing Mass Extinction, We Must Allow Ourselves to Grieve," Truthout, January 17, 2019, https://truthout.org/articles/in-facing-mass-extinction-we-dont-need-hope-we-need-to-grieve/#:
—:text=%E2%80%9CGrief%20requires%20us%20to%20-know,us%20to%20be%20hope%2Dfree.

PART TWO: DESCENT

1. Michael Meade, "The Vital Gradient Within Us," *Mosaic Voices*, https://www.mosaicvoices.org/the-vital-gradient-within-us
2. Michael Meade, *Fate and Destiny*, Greenfire Press, 2021.

8. DOORWAYS INTO DESCENT

1. Robert Johnson, *Understanding Masculine Psychology,* Harper Collins, 2009.

10. THE INESCAPABLE SHADOW

1. Connie Zweig, Jeremiah Abrams, *Meeting The Shadow*, Tarcher Press, 1991.

11. DARK SHADOW, BRIGHT SHADOW

1. Carl Jung, *Man and His Symbols*, New York, Dell Publishing, 1964.

12. 101 WAYS TO BYPASS THE SHADOW

1. Robert Augustus Masters, *Spiritual Bypassing: When Spirituality Disconnects Us from What Really Matters*, North Atlantic, 2010.

13. THE CULT OF INNOCENCE

1. Brené Brown, Richard Rohr, "Breathing Underwater, Falling Upward, Unlearning Certainty," Part 1, December 14, 2022, https://brenebrown.com/podcast/breathing-under-water-falling-upward-and-unlearning-certainty-part-1-of-2/?utm_medium=social&utm_source=Facebook&utm_campaign=bb_unlocking-us&fbclid=IwAR1yxasog4asIUFPwNcDDWwG4GX5hs2lPAwzuKnq8LLU_HEiBpp FJACF4jQ

14. WHAT SHADOW HEALING LOOKS LIKE

1. Debbie Ford, *The Dark Side of The Light-Chasers,* Riverhead Books, 2010.

15. DESCENT = GRIEF

1. Francis Weller, *Wisdom Bridge,* http://www.wisdombridge.net/the-reverence-of-approach.html

17. EVERYONE WE LOVE, WE WILL LOSE

1. Franz Kafka, *Selected Stories,* (ed. Nahum N. Glatzer). *The Complete Stories.* New York: Schocken Books, 1971.

18. THE PLACES THAT HAVE NOT KNOWN LOVE

1. You Tube: Brené Brown 2021 TED Talk, https://www.youtube.com/watch?v=psN1DORYYVo&t=652s

19. THE SORROWS OF THE WORLD

1. Andrew Harvey, *The Hope: A Guide to Sacred Activism,* Hay House, 2009.

20. WHAT WE EXPECTED BUT DID NOT RECEIVE

1. Rollo May, *Man's Search for Himself,* Norton, 1953.

2. "The Deep Ecology of the Sacred," *Catalyst Magazine*, September 30, 2019, https://catalystmagazine.net/the-deep-ecology-of-the-sacred/

21. ANCESTRAL GRIEF

1. "The Deep Ecology of the Sacred," *Catalyst Magazine*, September 30, 2019, https://catalystmagazine.net/the-deep-ecology-of-the-sacred/
2. Karina Margit Erdelyi, "Can Trauma Be Passed Down From One Generation to the Next?" August 31, 2022, https://www.psycom.net/trauma/epigenetics-trauma

22. DESCENT DOES NOT EQUAL DEPRESSION

1. "The Deep Ecology of The Sacred," *Catalyst Magazine*, September 30, 2019, https://catalystmagazine.net/the-deep-ecology-of-the-sacred/

23. GRIEF IS DOING ITS WORK IN YOU

1. Rainer Maria Rilke, *Letters to A Young Poet*, published by Leonard and Virginia Woolf at the Hogarth Press, 1932.
2. Carl Jung, *Man and His Symbols,* Doubleday, 1964.
3. *Ibid.*

24. A CULTURE IN DESCENT

1. William Catton, *Overshoot: The Ecological Basis of Revolutionary Change*, University of Illinois Press, 1982.
2. Mary Oliver, *Evidence*, Beacon Press, 2010.

PART THREE: JOY

1. Tim McKee, "An Interview With Francis Weller," North Atlantic Books, https://www.northatlanticbooks.com/blog/letter-from-the-publisher-an-interview-with-francis-weller-on-rituals-of-renewal/
2. William Blake, *Songs of Innocence and Experience*, 1794.

25. THE HAPPENSTANCE OF HAPPINESS

1. Rainer Maria Rilke, *Letters on Life*, edited and translated by Ulrich Baer, Modern Library, 2006.

26. BARRIERS ON THE ROAD TO JOY

1. Charles Upton, *Day and Night on the Sufi Path*, Sophia Perennis, 2015.
2. Joseph Campbell, *The Power of Myth*, Anchor Publishing, 1991.

27. RADICAL JOY FOR HARD TIMES

1. Radical Joy for Hard Times website, https://radicaljoy.org/radical-joy-revealed/sacred-filth/

RADICAL JOY PRACTICES

1. Radical Joy for Hard Times website, https://radicaljoy.org/ways-to-practice/

28. HOLDING THE TENSION OF LIFE'S OPPOSITES

1. Mark Nepo, *Inside The Miracle*, Sounds True Audio, 2016

29. BETWEEN HEARTBREAK AND ECSTASY

1. Henri J.M. Nouwen, "In Expectation," *Out of Solitude*, Ave Maria Press, 2004.

30. MAKING MEANING IN A TIME OF LOSS

1. Michael Meade, *Why the World Doesn't End: Tales of Renewal in Times of Loss*, Green Fire Press, 2012.

31. THE JOY OF MAKING MEANING

1. Robert Orsi, *Between Heaven and Earth: The Religious Worlds People Make and the Scholars Who Study Them*, Princeton University Press, 2006.

PART FOUR: CARING

1. "Leadership in Turbulent Times is Spiritual," Margaret Wheatley, 2002, https://www.margaretwheatley.com/articles/turbulenttimes.html

34. LARGE-SCALE CHANGE, SMALL-SCALE RELATIONSHIPS

1. How Large-Scale Change Really Happens," Meg Wheatley, https://www.margaretwheatley.com/articles/largescalechange.html
2. Ibid.

35. OCCUPY SPIRITUALITY

1. Andrew Harvey, *The Hope: A Guide to Sacred Activism*, Hay House, 2009
2. Occupy Spirituality: Prayer And Protest in the Age Of Trump, " *Science and Nonduality Website*, 2013, https://www.scienceandnonduality.com/article/occupy-spirituality-prayer-and-protest-in-the-age-of-trump
3. Ibid.

36. THE BODHISATTVA WARRIOR

1. Joanna Macy, "Allegiance To Live: Staying Steady Through The Mess We're In," *Tricycle Magazine*, 2012, https://tricycle.org/magazine/joanna-macy-interview/
2. Joanna Macy, "The Shambhala Warrior," *Awakin*, December, 2022, https://www.awakin.org/v2/read/view.php?tid=236
3. Ibid.

37. BECOMING A GOOD ANCESTOR

1. "Insights at the Edge," Tami Simon of Sounds True interviews Sobonfu Somé

38. CREATING A COUNTERCULTURE OF CARE

1. Kelly Hayes, "Activists are Building a Counterculture of Care in Apocalyptic Times," *Truthout*, 2020, https://truthout.org/audio/activists-are-building-a-counterculture-of-care-in-apocalyptic-times/

APPENDIX

1. *The Pocket Pema Chodron*, Shambhala Books, 2008.

ADDITIONAL RESOURCES

1. https://margaretwheatley.com/2020-europe-warriors-for-the-human-spirit-training/
2. https://www.soundstrue.com/products/the-healing-trauma-online-course
3. https://drgabormate.com/
4. https://integratedlistening.com/resource-center/?topic=576

www.ingramcontent.com/pod-product-compliance
Lightning Source LLC
Chambersburg PA
CBHW030603270326
41927CB00007B/1026